Computer Monographs

GENERAL EDITOR: Stanley Gill, M.A., Ph.D.
ASSOCIATE EDITOR: J. J. Florentin, Ph.D., Birkbeck College

Programs from Decision Tables

Programs from Decision Tables

E. Humby

Director of Studies
Systems Programming Organisation
International Computers Limited

Macdonald · London and
American Elsevier · New York

© E. Humby 1973

Sole distributors for the British Isles and Commonwealth
Macdonald & Co. (Publishers) Ltd.
49–50 Poland Street, London W.1

Sole distributors for the United States and Dependencies
American Elsevier Publishing Company Inc.
52 Vanderbilt Avenue, New York, N.Y. 10017

All remaining areas
Elsevier Publishing Company
P.O. Box 211, Jan van Galenstraat 335, Amsterdam, The Netherlands

Macdonald ISBN 0 356 04126 3
American Elsevier ISBN 0 444 19569 6
Library of Congress Catalog Card No 72 90803

Made and printed in Great Britain by
Balding + Mansell, London and Wisbech

Contents

1 The characteristics of decision tables

1.1 Introduction

One of the features of a well-designed program is the ease with which it can be modified. Ease of development corresponds closely to the systematic way the program was planned. The use of tables is often a hallmark of the systematic approach. This is because the elements of the table usually represent alternative values for parameters that can be used by a common piece of program in the several different situations. I can recall writing a tax routine which must have been one of the shortest (in number of instructions) ever written. It depended on a cunning use of the way the tax rates in each of three ranges related to each other. Alas, came the following April, and the routine had to be rewritten because the following year's tax rates were not so neatly related. Whilst the general process of summing tax at different rates over different ranges has remained the same over many years, the actual rates, the limits of the ranges, the number of ranges are liable to change from Budget to Budget. The preferred tax routine is one in which these items are contained in tables. It is then a simple process on Budget Day for someone without any knowledge of the working of the routine to provide a replacement table with every hope of success.

One strategy therefore in designing a program that is to be easily updated is to consider those aspects that are most liable to change and to arrange that they are the subject of tables that can easily be renewed. We shall see that decision tables are composed of conditions, data and actions, the principal elements of all programs, and for this reason can be used as an easily amendable device covering, not only data, but a large part of the logic of any program.

1

1.2 Producing a decision table

This book is concerned primarily with the translation of decision tables to computer programs and is not intended as a primer on the drafting of decision tables. The use of decision tables is amply described elsewhere. The Bibliography at the end of this book offers some examples. [2,3,4,7,8,9,19,23,24]. However, it might be useful to look in detail at one example first as a piece of revision if your reading on decision tables has not been recent, and second to establish a vocabulary for the various parts of the table. I have designed an example which makes fairly apparent the simplicity of the decision table approach compared with the procedural one.

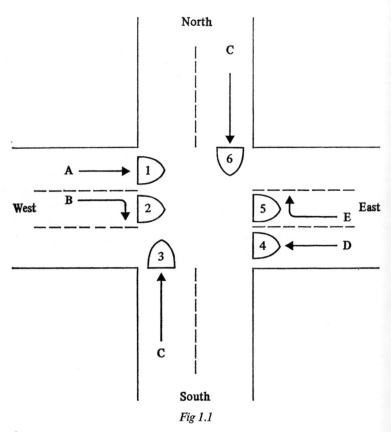

Fig 1.1

Let us apply ourselves to the problem of controlling the traffic lights at a road crossing (Fig. 1.1).

The road running east to west is a main one. At the crossing it has a centre lane for traffic turning right. The road is marked so that traffic in the two centre lanes can turn right together and the centre lanes have their own signal lights so that either they proceed together or one can proceed at the same time as its neighbour which is aiming straight ahead or turning left. The north-south road is not such a busy one and has no centre lane. Gadgets in the roads measure the separate queues A, B, C, D and E and produce a signal indicating whether they are short or long. Note that the north-south traffic is not allowed to turn right, and these two queues are both together called C, the gadget adding the queue lengths together.

Each queue has a STOP/GO signal. These are numbered 1 to 6 in the diagram.

The required program should repeatedly examine the state of the queues and at each examination decide which combination of signals to initiate. It is desirable that, in all the signal combinations for all the possible queue-state combinations, each queue should get a fair turn and each signal combination should appear, as far as is possible, as frequently as any other combination.

Note that it is sensible for the lights to give GO in pairs: 1 and 2, or 1 and 4, 4 and 5, 2 and 5, or 3 and 6.

It would certainly help sell the idea of decision tables if you would now spend 30 minutes (or more) trying to draw a flowchart for such a program. It will soon occur to you that some diagrammatic representation is required before one can start even on the flowchart. Such a diagram would be the one given in Fig. 1.2 which (as you might expect) is a decision table.

It consists of four sections. In the top left-hand one called the 'condition stub' we list the various conditions, in this case we name the queues. In the top-right section, called the 'condition body' we show different states of the conditions: an S stands for short and an L stands for long (given by the gadgets in the road). The bottom-left section is called the 'action stub' and names the possible actions, in this case each one indicates a particular signal that has to be switched to GO. The bottom-right section called the 'action body' is blank at the moment but later we shall be inserting Xs in the cells indicating 'switch this signal to GO'. (The absence of an X in this

Condition body

Condition stub

Fig. 1.2

	1	2	3	4	5	6	7	8	9	10	11	12	13	14	15	16	17	18	19	20	21	22	23	24	25	26	27	28	29	30	31	32
Queue A	S	S	S	S	S	S	S	S	S	S	S	S	S	S	S	S	L	L	L	L	L	L	L	L	L	L	L	L	L	L	L	L
Queue B	S	S	S	S	S	S	S	S	L	L	L	L	L	L	L	L	S	S	S	S	S	S	S	S	L	L	L	L	L	L	L	L
Queue C	S	S	S	S	L	L	L	L	S	S	S	S	L	L	L	L	S	S	S	S	L	L	L	L	S	S	S	S	L	L	L	L
Queue D	S	S	L	L	S	S	L	L	S	S	L	L	S	S	L	L	S	S	L	L	S	S	L	L	S	S	L	L	S	S	L	L
Queue E	S	L	S	L	S	L	S	L	S	L	S	L	S	L	S	L	S	L	S	L	S	L	S	L	S	L	S	L	S	L	S	L
Signal 1GO																																
Signal 2GO																																
Signal 3GO																																
Signal 4GO																																
Signal 5GO																																
Signal 6GO																																

Action stub

Action body

Fig. 1.3

	1	2	3	4	5	6	7	8	9	10	11	12	13	14	15	16	17	18	19	20	21	22	23	24	25	26	27	28	29	30	31	32
Queue A	S	S	S	S	S	S	S	S	S	S	S	S	S	S	S	S	L	L	L	L	L	L	L	L	L	L	L	L	L	L	L	L
Queue B	S	S	S	S	S	S	S	S	L	L	L	L	L	L	L	L	S	S	S	S	S	S	S	S	L	L	L	L	L	L	L	L
Queue C	S	S	S	S	L	L	L	L	S	S	S	S	L	L	L	L	S	S	S	S	L	L	L	L	S	S	S	S	L	L	L	L
Queue D	S	S	S	L	S	L	L	L	S	S	L	L	S	S	L	L	S	S	L	L	S	S	L	L	S	S	L	L	S	S	L	L
Queue E	S	L	S	L	S	L	L	L	S	L	S	L	S	L	S	L	S	L	S	L	S	L	S	L	S	L	S	L	S	L	S	L
Signal 1GO			X														X		X				X		X			X				
Signal 2GO		X							X	X															X				X			
Signal 3GO					X									X																		
Signal 4GO			X	X				X	X								X		X				X									
Signal 5GO		X		X				X	X	X				X																		
Signal 6GO					X																											

chart is taken to mean switch to STOP.) Each group of five indicators in each column of the condition body gives a possible combination of the queue states. Altogether 32 combinations (called rule identifiers) are given representing all possible combinations of the give queue states. This chart enables us systematically and thoroughly to consider each queue state and to decide in each case which pair of signals we shall switch to GO. The following reasoning leads us from the preceding diagram to the one after.

Some of the rule identifiers contain three short queues and two long queues and where the two long queues can happily proceed together it is very obvious that the signals in front of these long queues are the ones to be switched to GO (see columns 4, 10, 19, 25). We can use the same pairs where there are three long queues two of which can proceed together, the odd one being a competitor, namely C (see columns 8, 14, 23, 29).

Where in a rule identifier there is only one long queue, should it be C, then clearly 3 and 6 must be set to GO. If, however, it is A then we could set either 1 and 2, or 1 and 4 to GO. I have arbitrated 1 and 4 for A or D being long and 2 and 5 for B or E (see columns 2, 3, 5, 9, 17).

Fig. 1.3 gives the decision table as we have developed it so far.

It is clear that the signal pair 3 and 6 does not get a fair crack of the whip. What I shall do therefore to adjust the balance is to set 3 and 6 to GO wherever C is long in competition with one or two other queues (see columns 6, 7, 13, 15, 21, 22) or where C competes with three other long queues in which there is indecision because there are two pairs among the three competitors which are equally viable (for instance columns 16, 24, 30, 31). The action part of the table now looks like Fig 1.4.

Since two signals will be set in each of 32 columns finally we can see that there will be 64 Xs in all. 64 does not divide exactly by 6, so a reasonable distribution would be one in which the row total of Xs was 11 in four cases and 10 in the other two. 3 and 6 have therefore now got their fair ration. But now let us look at the frequency with which we have used the signal pairs. The score so far is as follows:

1 and 2	–	2 times	1 and 4	–	4 times
4 and 5	–	2 times	2 and 5	–	4 times
3 and 6	–	11 times			

Fig. 1.4

	1	2	3	4	5	6	7	8	9	10	11	12	13	14	15	16	17	18	19	20	21	22	23	24	25	26	27	28	29	30	31	32	
Signal 1GO			X														X		X				X		X			X					6
Signal 2GO		X							X	X				X											X			X					6
Signal 3GO					X	⊗							⊗			⊗				⊗	⊗			⊗						⊗	⊗		11
Signal 4GO			X	X				X	X								X		X				X										6
Signal 5GO		X		X				X	X					X											X			X					6
Signal 6GO					X	⊗							⊗			⊗				⊗	⊗			⊗						⊗	⊗		11

Fig. 1.5

	1	2	3	4	5	6	7	8	9	10	11	12	13	14	15	16	17	18	19	20	21	22	23	24	25	26	27	28	29	30	31	32
Queue A	S	S	S	S	S	S	S	S	L	L	L	S	S	S	S	S	S	L	L	L	L	L	L	L	L	L	L	L	L	L	L	L
Queue B	S	S	S	S	S	S	S	L	L	L	L	L	L	L	L	L	L	S	S	S	S	S	S	S	S	L	L	S	L	L	L	L
Queue C	S	S	S	S	L	L	L	L	L	S	S	S	L	L	L	L	S	S	S	S	S	L	L	L	S	L	S	S	S	L	L	L
Queue D	S	S	L	L	S	S	S	L	S	S	L	S	L	S	L	S	S	S	L	L	L	S	L	L	S	S	S	L	S	S	S	L
Queue E	L	L	S	L	S	L	S	L	S	L	S	L	S	L	S	L	L	L	S	L	S	L	S	L	S	L	S	L	L	S	L	L
Signal 1GO			X								⊗						X	⊗					X		X	⊗			X		L	⊗
Signal 2GO	⊗	X							X	X	⊗		X				X						X		X	⊗			X		L	
Signal 3GO	X			X	X	X	X							X	X	X			X		X	X		X						X	X	
Signal 4GO		X	X	X				X	X	X		⊗								⊗							⊗	⊗				⊗
Signal 5GO	⊗	X		X		X	X	X	X	X		⊗	X	X	X	X	X		X	⊗	X	X	X	X								⊗
Signal 6GO					X	X	X						X		X	X					X			X						X	X	

Any pair will do for rule 1 (all short queues) or rule 32 (all long queues) so they can be left till last for use as make-weights. The first blank rule is then 11. We can satisfy queue B with a 1 and 2 or with a 2 and 5. I have chosen 1 and 2 because this pair is currently under-utilised. Choices are made for the remaining blanks on this basis of balancing up the frequency of use. Don't worry about the frequency of 11 for the pair 3 and 6. That is because two queues are labelled C. After this stage we find we can use 2 and 5 for columns 1 and 32 and that completes the decision table. The completed table is shown in Fig 1.5.

The number of Xs against each signal is either 10 or 11 and the frequency of the signal pairs is as equitable as anyone could get it.

Signal 1	–	10	1 and 2	–	5 times
2	–	11	4 and 5	–	5 times
3	–	11	3 and 6	–	11 times
4	–	10	1 and 4	–	5 times
5	–	11	2 and 4	–	6 times
6	–	11			32
		64			

To complete a program we must get this decision table translated into a procedure by one of the means described in later chapters, and we must add a control routine which examines the state of the queues at appropriate intervals and somehow switches the lights. We must observe that we are dealing with a problem in real time and it is very likely that in this field we shall more and more frequently be faced with problems involving numerous combinations of circumstances none of which must be missed. The example shows how easily a decision table forces attention to all the possibilities. Consider moreover how simple the task of changing the bias would be – if for instance the use of the north south route increased. And how much more difficult such a change would be to a flowchart representation of the problem.

1.3 Types of table

Before examining the methods of translation of decision tables into computer programs let us look at the different types and the several attributes which they may possess. The literature on the subject refers to 'limited entry' and 'extended entry'. The former is always fairly clearly defined but the latter term is often used loosely. We shall seek some clarification for the purposes of this book. It is possible so to frame the terms in the condition stub as to constitute a Boolean with only two possible states, True and False. These states are indicated in the condition body conventionally by Y and N, respectively, meaning Yes and No. The term 'extended entry' is loosely used for any other type of filling. Conveniently, the stub could contain a question with several possible answers one of which was used in each cell in the body. This frequently leads to misunderstandings. Consider for example the following as a row in a decision table describing a problem in spectroscopy.

WAVEBAND? RED YELLOW BLUE GREEN

The range of wavelengths implied by the word 'red' will need additional clarification. There can be no guarantee that all possible wavelengths are covered or that some wavelengths are not covered by two of the terms. This must be regarded as sloppy practice and tables of this sort will not be discussed further. Note, however, that the following row from a decision table describing play in a game of Ludo is perfectly acceptable.

WHOSE GO? RED YELLOW BLUE GREEN

Here the terms satisfy the criteria of all good sets in that they are mutually exclusive and collectively exhaustive.

Definition will be easier if we separate the question of format from the question of the number of states which each condition may attain. It will be convenient in discussing decision tables to consider tables in which the conditions have two possible states from those that have more than two. The two-state kind I shall call 'limited entry', whether the two are represented by Y and N, or Yes and No, or 0 and 1, or, for that matter, White and Black. The multistate kind I shall call 'extended entry' and you can assume that this implies the various states are mutually exclusive and collectively exhaustive, unless otherwise stated.

A good practice adopted by many systems analysts in the case of extended entry is to carefully compose the list of possibilities, then number them and use the numbers in the body of the decision table.

We shall be using this numerical method often because in discussing methods of handling tables we may not be very interested in what the actual individual numbers mean.

1.4 Completeness

One of the advantages of using the decision table layout is that it enables us to examine systematically each possible combination of conditions to make sure that at the end no possibility has been missed. The following examples of first a limited and secondly an extended entry table show how the rules can be systematically drawn.

```
C1   N N N N Y Y Y Y
C2   N N Y Y N N Y Y
C3   N Y N Y N Y N Y
```

```
C1   1 1 1 1 1 1 1 1 2 2 2 2 2 2 2 2 3 3 3 3 3 3 3 3   3 possibilities
C2   1 1 1 1 2 2 2 2 1 1 1 1 2 2 2 2 1 1 1 1 2 2 2 2   2 possibilities
C3   1 2 3 4 1 2 3 4 1 2 3 4 1 2 3 4 1 2 3 4 1 2 3 4   4 possibilities
```

In the first case where there are two possibilities for each of three conditions, the number of rules is $2^3 = 8$. More generally for the limited entry table the number of possible rules is 2^n, where n is the number of conditions. Examining the numerical extended entry table we see there are 24 different rules. The 24 is given by multiplying together the number of possibilities for each of the conditions: $3 \times 2 \times 4 = 24$. This rule of multiplying the numbers of possibilities holds good, of course, for the limited case as well. It is, then, an easy matter for a decision table preprocessor (human or program) to verify the total number of possible rules and check whether the proffered table is complete or not.

1.5 Abbreviation

Writing down all the possible rules for large tables can be a tedious operation. I have not heard of a program (but it would certainly be useful) which will output a complete table so that the analyst has only to consider the actions in each case. But if the actions are the same for many of the rules even this will appear onerous. There are two common ways in which the task can be abbreviated and we will examine what effect each has on our evaluation of completeness.

One method is the use of a symbol, conventionally the dash, to mean that the particular state of the condition is irrelevant to the rule. For example, below on the left are two columns of a limited entry decision table.

C1	Y Y		C1	Y
C2	N N		C2	N
C3	N Y		C3	–
C4	Y Y		C4	Y
A1			A1	
A2	X X		A2	X
A3			A3	
A4	X X		A4	X

You can see that the state of condition 3 is immaterial since in either case actions 2 and 4 will be obeyed. By the use of the dash we can draw these two columns as one as on the right.

Each dash in a limited entry decision table means that two rules have been combined into one. If the limited entry table has a rule containing n dashes then that one rule is replacing 2^n separate rules. Dashes can be similarly used in extended entry tables but in that case a rule containing a dash is replacing p rules, where p is the number of possible states for the appropriate condition. If there are several dashes in one rule then the number of rules represented is the product of the various p possibilities. Below are shown the condition parts of several decision tables where the number at the foot of each column indicates the number of separate rules replaced by that single abbreviated rule. Notice that in each case we can calculate the number of rules required for a complete table and compare it with the number of rules represented. The use of the dash does not prevent a completeness test.

C1	Y Y N N	Total possible	$2 \times 2 \times 2 \times 2 = 16$
C2	– N – Y	No. represented	$4 + 1 + 4 + 2 = 11$
C3	N Y – –		
C4	– N Y N		Table is incomplete
	4 1 4 2		

C1	Y N Y – N	Total possible	$2 \times 2 \times 2 = 8$
C2	N – Y N Y	No. represented	$1 + 2 + 2 + 2 + 1 = 8$
C3	Y Y – N N		Table is complete
	1 2 2 2 1		

C1	1 2 – 1 4 4 2 3 4 1 3 1 1 2 3 3	Total possible	$4 \times 2 \times 3 = 24$
C2	2 1 1 2 1 2 1 2 1 2 – 1 1 2 2 1	No. represented	$= 24$
C3	1 3 1 2 3 – 3 1 2 3 2 3 2 – 3 3		Table is complete
	. . . .		
	1 1 4 1 1 3 1 1 1 1 2 1 1 3 1 1		

A second method of abbreviation is the use of an ELSE rule. Consider the case of a decision table which explains what has to be done in a program which validates data. The field containing the record type might be a two-digit numeric, and the valid types for this particular program might be 45, 67, 84 and 87, any other type number being an error. It is clearly undesirable to write 100 rules for all possible types when 96 of them will all lead to a common error routine. Similar arguments might apply to other attributes of the data such that the valid cases may represent only a few per cent of the total combinations. The convention adopted in such cases is to draft only those rules which correspond to valid cases and then to have a dummy rule on the right which is understood to represent 'all other possibilities'. This dummy rule is known as the ELSE rule. Here is an example

																		ELSE
Col. 1 contains	1	1	1	1	1	1	2	2	2	2	2	2	3	3	3	3	3	3
Col. 2 contains	M	M	M	F	F	F	M	M	M	F	F	F	M	M	M	F	F	F
Cols. 8 & 9 contains	19	20	21	19	20	21	19	20	21	19	20	21	19	20	21	19	20	21
Set bonus =	32	33	34	35	36	37	38	39	40	41	42	43	44	45	46	47	48	49	00
Go to ERROR																			X

Any record in which col. 1 is not 1, 2 or 3, col. 2 is not M or F, or cols. 8 & 9 are not 19, 20 or 21 will cause 'bonus' to be set zero and the program switched to an error routine.

11

1.6 Checking completeness

Now consider completeness. By definition a decision table with an ELSE rule covers all cases since any rule is either stated explicitly or is implied by the ELSE rule. However, it is quite possible that the drafter forgot a particular valid case, and by default such a case will lead to the ELSE rule and cause the error routine to be obeyed. Unlike abbreviation by dashes therefore, the use of the ELSE rule puts the onus of completeness on the drafter and the processor is unable to warn him of suspected omissions.

1.7 Ambiguity

The extensive use of dashes increases the risk of 'ambiguity' and a good processor should apply checks that ambiguity has not occured. In the following example, two rules of a decision table lead to different actions. Suppose that the particular key being set against the table is the one shown on the right.

	Rule 1 2 3 4 5 6 7 8		
C1	Y –		Y
C2	– N		N
C3	– Y		Y
C4	Y Y		Y
Send Free sample	X		
Offer discount	X		
Send literature		X	
Send agent later		X	

Either rule 4 or rule 6 satisfies the key and it is not known whether action 4 or 6 is the correct one. This type of ambiguity is called a 'contradiction'. Consider a similar case except that the two rules lead to the same action. Since the omission of either one of the rules would not affect the result as far as the given key is concerned, we regard this form of ambiguity as a 'redundancy'.

	Rule 1 2 3 4 5 6 7 8	
C1	Y –	Y
C2	– N	N
C3	– Y	Y
C4	Y Y	Y
Send Free Sample	X X	
Offer discount		
Send literature	X X	
Send agent later	X X	

A decision table is free of ambiguity provided that between any one rule and any other there is a Y/N distinction in at least one of the condition rows. It must be pointed out at this stage that some cases which appear as ambiguities by the above considerations may not be real ambiguities if we take into account the actual meanings of the conditions and the states. Take, for example, the following three rows from a limited entry, decision table (Fig 1.6).

C1 Height < 5 ft	Y	–	–	
C2 Height 5 ft to 6 ft	–	Y	–	
C3 Height > 6 ft	–	–	Y	

Fig. 1.6

Our test for completeness shows that there should be $2 \times 2 \times 2 = 8$ possibilities. However, we know from our understanding of the conditions that it is impossible for any real situation to give a Yes in more than one position of the key. It could be tricky to have a program processor distinguish between real and apparent ambiguities without special help from the drafter. (Though King has given this problem much thought [13], [14].) It could be argued that this situation only arises because we have been bending the limited entry table to do something that could best be done using an extended entry. If we declare in a 'condition list' the three height ranges to be three states of a single condition then the three rows of the previous

Ranges		
< 5 ft	= 1	
5 ft to 6 ft	= 2	
> 6 ft	= 3	

C1 Height range	1	2	3		

Fig. 1.7

example become a single condition row having three possible states (Fig 1.7). This enables a processor to apply completeness tests but puts the onus on the drafter to be sure that his possibilities are mutually exclusive and collectively exhaustive.

The reader may feel at this point that the distinction between limited and extended entry decision tables which persists in much of the literature on this subject is a little artificial and that a more general approach could be applied to some of the features of decision tables if we handled them all as extended entry numeric format. This often would make unnecessary the specific use of the ELSE rule, for instance, by having the last member of all our condition lists represent 'all other values of this condition'. What we have been calling limited entry then becomes just the particular case in which each condition has one element standing for one special value and a second element standing for any other state. There is little doubt that the unnatural stress on the limited entry, Y/N table derives from the fact that a processing program is simpler if confined to such cases, particularly if the hardware processor has binary logic instructions. (On detecting ambiguities at run-time with application to extended entry, see [18].)

2 Decision tables to computer programs

2.1 Conversion

Now to get down to the problems of converting decision tables into computer programs. Perhaps first it should be emphasised that only a small fraction of decision tables get converted to computer programs by program processors. Decision tables are often used to define a piece of logic for the benefit of people who have to make decisions depending on various circumstances, where resolution at computers' speeds may not be necessary. They may be income tax assessors, national assistance officers, insurance claim examiners, etc. Furthermore, many systems analysts use decision tables to describe systems to programmers, primarily for the clarity they encourage though neither have the intention to convert to computer program automatically. This may be because decision tables are not the most suitable means of describing every part of every program or because the programmer is sceptical about the efficiency of object programs produced by software processors. It can only be hoped that the procedures described in this book help such programmers to assess the appropriateness of decision tables for their work, help them produce quicker and more efficient programs from decision table descriptions, and enable them the better to evaluate different software processors so that decisions to use or not use are made without prejudice.

Conditions, rule identifiers and actions must all be expressed in some language understood by analyst, programmer and, in the case of automatic translation, by the computer, and this implies for the processor a syntax analysis capability. Since there already exist programming languages and their translators there is no particular

15

need to create more problems by specifying any different languages for use with decision tables. Program processors for decision tables therefore frequently concern themselves only with the task of transforming the logic expressed by the table into the procedural form of program required by current computers. To the extent that they can treat the actual wording of the conditions and actions as mere strings of characters without understanding their meaning, they can output a program in an acceptable programming language and leave a proprietary compiler to complete the translation into machine code. We shall usually find therefore that decision table translators come in the form of preprocessors to the popular high level language compilers COBOL, FORTRAN, and ALGOL. A converter in Algol is given.[6]

Certainly in this book I shall confine our attention to the processing of the logic, and having described means of converting to flowchart form shall assume that the reader already knows the route from there to machine code or can find out from another source.

2.2 The long way

Let us begin with the most straightforward, but quite inefficient, translation of a decision table into procedural form. A bonus is to be paid to all employees with more than 10 years' service. Preference is to be given to employees over the age of 50 and men get more than women (Fig 2.1).

	1	2	3	4	5	6	7	8
Service > 10 years	Y	Y	Y	Y	N	N	N	N
Sex = Male	Y	Y	N	N	Y	Y	N	N
Age > 50	Y	N	Y	N	Y	N	Y	N
Pay Bonus of	90	70	80	60	0	0	0	0

Fig. 2.1

16

By reading from top to bottom and left to right we could compose a COBOL program which went like this

IF SERVICE > 10 AND SEX = M AND AGE >
    50 MOVE 90 TO BONUS.
IF SERVICE > 10 AND SEX = M AND AGE NOT >
    50 MOVE 70 TO BONUS.
IF SERVICE > 10 AND SEX NOT = M AND AGE >
    50 MOVE 80 TO BONUS.
IF SERVICE > 10 AND SEX NOT = M AND AGE NOT >
    50 MOVE 60 TO BONUS.
IF SERVICE < 10 AND SEX = M AND AGE >
    50 MOVE ZERO TO BONUS.
    etc.

Since the conditions are fairly simple there is no overwhelming inefficiency but the condition regarding service might have been more complicated; ' . . . service will be reduced by any period of illness greater than two months. Overseas service can be counted double provided that such periods of service exceed three months. Separate periods of service may be accumulated. Service with the XYZ Co. prior to its takeover will count for only half. A month is defined . . . etc'.

2.3 Rule matching

It would not be practical to write out the equivalent test program eight times and one would normally write a subroutine which recorded a Yes or No signal according to whether the resultant service was greater than ten years or not. Let us suppose that we resolve each of the conditions for any one employee storing the result as Y or N, then we can form a key for that employee. In the case of a 55-year-old woman with 23 years' service the key would be YNY. We can compare this key with each rule identifier in turn and we discover a match on rule 3. The action associated with that rule causes an award of an £80 bonus. The advantage of this method over the previous program is that the instructions for testing each condition are stored once only and are obeyed once only for each employee. There are a few additional instructions to form the key and to search the decision table.

It is interesting to examine what happens if we substitute an 0 for Yes and a 1 for No (Fig. 2.2)

Service > 10 yrs	0	0	0	0	1	1	1	1
Sex = Male	0	0	1	1	0	0	1	1
Age > 50	0	1	0	1	0	1	0	1
Pay Bonus of	90	70	80	60	0	0	0	0

Fig. 2.2

Each rule identifier is a binary number which in a binary address computer could be used directly to extract the bonus, in this case from a table of bonuses without even the need to store all the rule identifiers. Alas the above trick is only applicable if the decision table is (a) complete and (b) limited entry.

The ability to create a unique number which leads to the appropriate action paragraph prompted Veinott[26] to propose a method in which a decision table could be resolved by two COBOL instructions

COMPUTE JUMP $= 1 + C1 + C2*2 + C3*4 \ldots$

GO TO N1, N2, N3 ... DEPENDING ON JUMP

where $Cn = 1$ if the nth condition gives Y and 0 if it gives N. This device can be modified for incomplete and extended entry.

2.4 Rule Masking

Let us go back to the earlier device where we built up the key to see what happens if the table is abbreviated. First suppose the table has an ELSE rule. This would mean a simple extension to the program so that having examined all the specific rule identifiers without finding a match then the program would direct us to the action given at the foot of the ELSE rule. Things are a little more complicated if dashes appear in the table. If the table were stored with Y and N indicators then before the key is compared with a rule

18

identifier it will need to be modified by having a dash replace any Y or N where the rule identifier had a dash in the corresponding position.

R1	R2	R3	R4	R5	R6	R7	ELSE	
N	N	N	Y	Y	–	–		
N	–	–	–	–	Y	Y		Table 1
N	Y	N	–	–	N	–		
N	N	Y	N	Y	Y	N		

1	1	1	1	1	0	0	
1	0	0	0	0	1	1	
1	1	1	0	0	1	0	Table 2
1	1	1	1	1	1	1	

0	0	0	1	1	0	0	
0	0	0	0	0	1	1	
0	1	0	0	0	0	0	Table 3
0	0	1	0	1	1	0	

Again, this can be done quite neatly where the computer has binary logic operations. The first table in Fig. 2.3 represents a decision table in Y N form with dashes. The second table is a binary table with a 0 for every dash and a 1 for every non-dash, that is a specific Y or N. The third table is a binary one with a 1 in every position in which there was a Y in the first one and a 0 for every non-Y, that is a N or a dash. Now our program will have to resolve each condition and form a key. If the results were NYNY in order we should form a key 0101. What we must then do is perform a logical ANDing of this key with the first mask in Table 2. ANDing 0101 with 1111 gives 0101. This result is compared with the first identifier in Table 3 and in this case is seen not to match. We repeat the process for each identifier in turn until after ANDing with Table 2 we get a match with Table 3. Our particular key 0101 will succeed on R3 where ANDing with 1011 gives 0001 which matches.

This is called 'Rule Masking' and is attributed to Kirk.[15] A modification to avoid testing every condition is proposed by King.[11] Other means of improving the method are suggested by Barnard[1] and Woodall.[27]

2.5 Sequential branching

In the masking method we have been examining, it is not too difficult to make an assessment about costs. Each reference to the table requires at run time that each condition must be tested. Now suppose that one of the rules in a table looked like this

    C1 –
    C2 Y
    C3 –
    C4 –

then a single test of condition 2 could, if the answer was Yes, lead us directly to the actions to be obeyed. Let us then think about replacing the condition half of the table with a flowchart of condition tests that lead to the various actions to see if we can capitalise on shortening the run time use of the decision table.

The decision table in Fig. 2.3 is logically equivalent to the flow chart shown below it.

C1 Y Y Y Y N N N N
C2 Y Y N N Y Y N N
C3 Y N Y N Y N Y N

A B C D E F G H

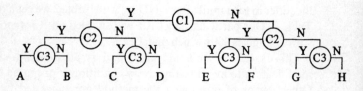

Fig. 2.3

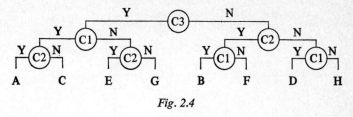

Fig. 2.4

Note that the flowchart in Fig. 2.4 is also logically equivalent and there are others which you could think up for yourself.

However, we must make this observation about them all: any run-time path through the table has to obey three condition tests and that is no better than the masking method. It is even worse from the storage point of view in that the flowchart shows that seven tests must be stored away in memory. Using the rule mask method only three tests would be required for this decision table.

What was different about the rule given earlier that tempted us to think there was something to be gained was that the rule contained several dashes. Take a look at the following decision table which is well blessed with dashes. (The last rule leading to action Z is an ELSE rule.)

```
C1   Y N N .
C2   - Y N .
C3   - Y - .
     A B C Z
```

Fig. 2.5 shows an equivalent flowchart

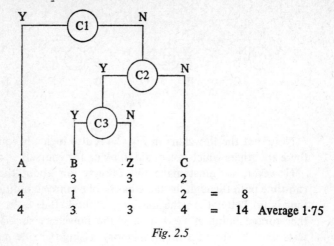

A	B	Z	C		
1	3	3	2		
4	1	1	2	=	8
4	3	3	4	=	14 Average 1·75

Fig. 2.5

Only three tests need to be stored – no worse than by rule masking. There are none of the overheads of rule masking. Of the eight possible keys four lead to A through a path with only one test, one leads to B through three tests and one to Z through three tests. Two keys lead to C through two tests. The eight possible keys need 14 tests to identify them. That means the average run time is only 1·75 tests long and that is very much better than by rule masking.

In the next chapters we shall examine more closely the production of such flowcharts.

3 On the generality of decision tables

3.1 The mechanism for converting to flowchart

Let us get used to the way a decision table breaks down into a flowchart.

```
C1  Y N N .
C2  - Y N .
C3  - Y - .

    A B C Z
```

Taking C1 at random for resolution first

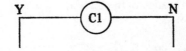

For simplicity let us adopt the convention that Yes is the left-hand branch and No is the right-hand branch, as later I shall omit the Y and N indicators on the branches. Examining the decision table it is clear that if C1 gives Y then action A must be performed no matter what the result of condition 2 or 3. However, if C1 gives N then we are really left with a part of the decision table still to translate. The position at this stage can be represented

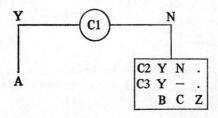

Let us then take the next condition, C2 as the next test on the No branch from the C1 test. If the answer on C2 test is No then without more ado action C is called for, but if C2 test gives Yes then we still have a bit of the decision table left.

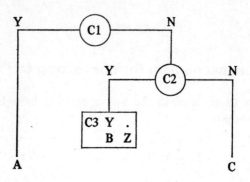

The completion of the translation is given by putting a test of C3 in the Yes branch of the C2 test.

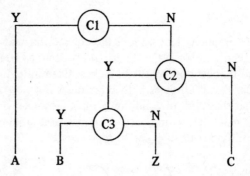

For a second example take the same decision table but suppose that condition 2 had been chosen as the one to be tested first. This would have left a sub-table on each branch

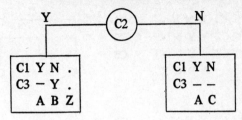

Taking C1 as the next test in the No branch it can be seen that a Yes gives action A and No gives action C. Taking C1 as the next test in the Yes branch of the C2 test, however, calls for some further resolution.

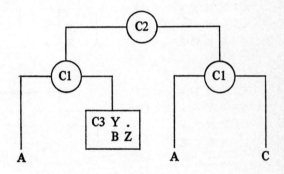

This can be completed

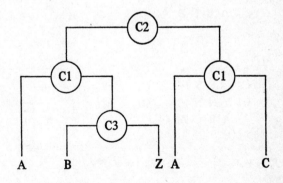

25

1   C1 Y N N ·   C1
      C2 − Y N ·   C2
      C3 − Y − ·   C3
         A B C Z

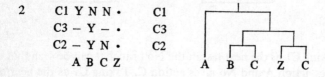

2   C1 Y N N ·   C1
      C3 − Y − ·   C3
      C2 − Y N ·   C2
         A B C Z

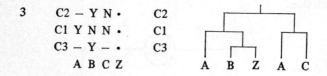

3   C2 − Y N ·   C2
      C1 Y N N ·   C1
      C3 − Y − ·   C3
         A B C Z

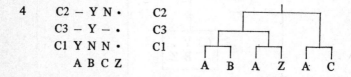

4   C2 − Y N ·   C2
      C3 − Y − ·   C3
      C1 Y N N ·   C1
         A B C Z

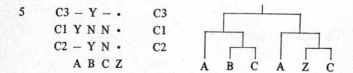

5   C3 − Y − ·   C3
      C1 Y N N ·   C1
      C2 − Y N ·   C2
         A B C Z

6   C3 − Y − ·   C3
      C2 − Y N ·   C2
      C1 Y N N ·   C1
         A B C Z

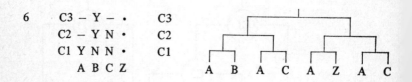

Fig. 3.1

3.2 A multiplicity of charts

We have developed two flowcharts from the one decision table. They are the same logically, that is to say on any single assumption of the state of the three conditions we are led to the same action whichever of the charts we use. However, they are different in form, for example we would be storing three tests in one case but four tests in the other. The difference arises simply because of the sequence in which we chose to make the tests. Fig. 3.1 shows six different flowcharts all logically equivalent to the same original decision table. The decision table shown on the left in each case is the same one;

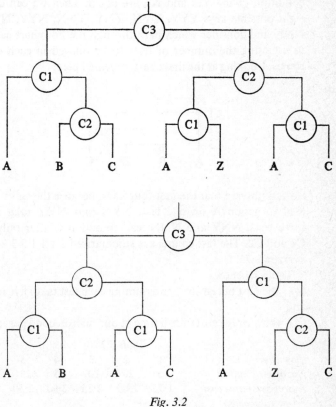

Fig. 3.2

I have merely switched the rows so that you can more easily follow the logic. The two examples we worked in detail are numbers one and three. A branch to the left is Yes and a branch to the right is No. Fig. 3.2 shows two more also equivalent, making eight in all.

3.3 Choosing the 'best' chart

Let us consider all these flowcharts from the points of view of
(a)   number of tests to be stored,
(b)   average run time resolution.
There are three tests stored in the best case and seven in the worst. To measure average run time let us suppose that the chances of any condition giving Yes and No are equal. Then we can consider the eight possible keys YYY, YYN, YNY, YNN, NYY, NYN, NNY, NNN and consider which path through the flowchart each will lead us counting the number of tests to be obeyed in each of the eight routes. Looking at the first chart, repeated here,

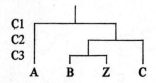

we can observe that the first four keys, because they give Yes for C1, lead to action A on one test. NYN and NYY take us through three tests. NNY and NNN lead to action C after only two tests, C1 and C2. The test counts are summarised 1 1 1 1 3 3 2 2, total 14, average 1·75.

Table 3.1 shows
(a)   the cost of test storage assuming each test takes five instructions, and
(b)   the average cost of run time at one microsecond per instruction.

Table 3.1

Flow chart No.	1	2	3	4	5	6
No. of instructions	15	20	20	25	25	35
Average run time cost (microseconds)	1·75	2·00	2·25	2·50	2·50	3·00

28

Now let us suppose that the situation is not quite as equitable as we have so far assumed: that, for example, the number of instructions in the different condition tests vary widely and that some keys in real life have a much greater probability than others. We might find that flowchart 3 rather than 1 is the best in respect of storage cost and that flowchart 4 is better than 1 regarding run time cost. We must treat with suspicion therefore any claim that a particular flowchart equivalent is the 'best' unless the facts about condition cost and probability of key are known and the relative importance of these two criteria is also given.

3.4 A key to the next steps in automatic programming

I should like at this point to postpone discussion of the development of methods for translation of decision tables to programs and consider the significance of what the preceding exercise has shown about the relative standing of decision tables and flowcharts. Both of them are means of expressing program logic. They both contain condition tests and actions. And yet for one decision table we found eight equivalent flowcharts. The decision table must then be a more general way of expressing the logic than any one of the charts. The reason may now be easy to see. Each flowchart makes some assumption about the precedence of the condition tests, whereas the decision table makes no such assumption. If a problem is described in English and a programmer constructs a computer program for it by first drawing a flowchart (a very common practice) then we are entirely in the hands of that programmer as to whether we get the 'best' flowchart out of the many possible. It must also be true of course that if we spell out the problem as a decision table then we are in the hands of the decision table processor what kind of a program results. If this processor is automatic, that is a software one, then that software can be designed and refined to maximise on some criteria. It is one of the objects of this book to explore the feasibility of such optimisation.

The history of automatic programming has proceeded in jerks. I can remember a time when instructions for the computer were punched in binary and the thrill of first using a thing called a loader which enabled the numeric form which we used in our preliminary

29

planning to be translated automatically. We foresaw that one day the instructions might even be presented to the computer with mnemonic names for the functions and addresses. We told the prophets who claimed that one day the computer would print out a program in something very like English that we would believe that when we actually saw it. Nevertheless the thought that the programmer's own job would gradually be made more and more automatic was an exciting one.

After the loaders came the assemblers and then macros and then FORTRAN and COBOL and then – a long pause. The pause, of course, was because the idea of languages was getting ahead of the hardware, just about one generation ahead. But, alas, when the third generation of computers offered the performance necessary for the practical translation of a second generation language like COBOL, the programming fraternity had lost the taste for automatic programming and had turned their interest to other things, leaving this field incomplete. We have since had PL/1; but whilst this undoubtedly broadens the front of the attack on automatic programming it fails to make any very much deeper penetration of the problem.

We have just come to the conclusion that decision tables possess a greater generality than flowcharts and therefore than procedural languages like COBOL, FORTRAN, ALGOL or PL/1. I call these languages procedural because the person who writes a program in them determines the way in which the statements proceed from one to the other. The decision table makes no such assumptions but leaves the sequence of events to be determined separately by possibly an automatic and, hopefully, an optimising process.

One remarkable fact is that in all the eulogising of decision tables you will seldom find much mention of this most important role of decision tables (it was pointed out by King[12] in '67). If indeed decision tables are the key to a major advance in automatic programming then this aspect overshadows the many other advantages which they may offer to the systems analyst and the programmer. Decision tables have been a long time in labour. (A programming language based on decision table logic was, however, proposed in 1964 by Lombardi.[16])

One of the earliest articles on such tables was by Evans[28] although similar things called truth tables were in common use by elec-

30

tronic engineers and others. From time to time someone, even CODASYL [5,10] have got excited about them but it cannot be said that even today decision tables are in common use.

This hesitant approach has in its turn developed an unhealthy respect for the conventions. Many would be as shocked by the suggestion of putting anything other than an X to indicate 'this action is to be performed' as they would at a proposal that something other than X represents a draw on their football coupon. This kind of rigidity has put a straitjacket on a vigorous development of decision tables. They are frequently presented as nothing more than a neat little device for expressing a bit of logic. Perhaps if more flexibility were accepted in format and representation their undoubted generality could be fully exploited in getting us all on the road again of programming automation. This book will have accomplished something if it can at least have pointed the way.

4 Conversion guaranteeing a best solution

4.1 The real cost of a guaranteed best

In the last chapter we saw that for any given decision table there are several flowchart equivalents some better than others according to the criteria we set. The translation has control of which flowchart it produces by governing the sequence in which it chooses to evaluate the conditions. The secret we are searching for therefore is the rule by which we choose the next condition test. The literature on decision tables offers a number of tactics. All too often their authors put them forward as the tactic which gives the best answer. Invariably another author shows a case where that solution is a long way from best and then puts forward a tactic of his own. He in turn comes under a similar attack. We shall examine some of these tactics later because they are practical contributions to the game but that they are makeshifts in place of the ultimate best is never explained.

We have seen that given the criteria we can recognise the best answer. The logical approach is to start with the most patent solution and that is 'generate all the possible flowchart equivalents, evaluate each in terms of storage requirement and/or average run time and output the one which looks best according to the criteria'. As you probably expected life is not going to be as simple as that and the reason is that in all but the smallest cases this task would take us far too long.

For an appreciation of just how big a task we are talking about let us consider first the smallest meaningful decision table, a limited entry one with two conditions.

$$\begin{array}{llll} \text{C1} & \text{Y Y N N} \\ \text{C2} & \text{Y N Y N} \\ & \phantom{\text{Y}} 1 \ 2 \ 3 \ 4 \end{array}$$

There are two possible flowchart equivalents. These are shown in Fig. 4.1.

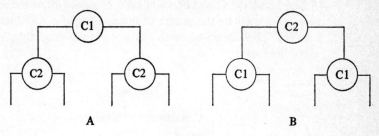

A

B

Fig. 4.1

For convenience call these type A and type B. Now consider the next level of decision table with three conditions. All the possible flowcharts will have a common form shown in Fig 4.2.

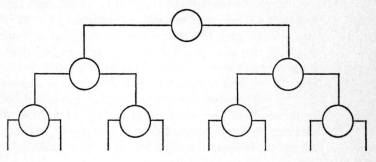

Fig. 4.2

They will differ only by the condition numbers in the circles. We can regard such a flowchart as a single condition test with a level two format hung on each branch. The numbering of the conditions in each of the level two formats is either type A or type B. There is the possibility of three conditions for the first test making in all $2 \times 2 \times 3 = 12$ possibilities.

Continuing the argument we can foresee that the level four format will be a single test with a level three format hanging from each of the two branches. Each of those level three formats, as we have just

33

calculated, has 12 possible numberings and the test at the head has four possibilities. This gives in all $12 \times 12 \times 4 = 576$ possibilities.

In general, then, for a decision table of n conditions the number of possibilities will be the square of the number of possibilities at level $n-1$ multiplied by n and on this basis the following table, Table 4.1, is constructed.

Table 4.1

Conditions	Flowcharts
2	2
3	12
4	576
5	1 658 880
3	$16\,513 \times 10^9$
7	19×10^{26}

Seven conditions cannot be regarded as producing a large decision table but it is clearly unreasonable to generate 19×10^{26} flowcharts and evaluate each one to discover the best. But it is one thing to recognise that there is a best that is impractical of attainment and quite another thing to make wild stabs at a solution believing it to produce the best until someone comes along to disprove it. Our 'find'em all' algorithm might be operable in small decision tables or for resolving partial subsets of an original decision table where solution by more straightforward techniques suggested several candidates for next condition test as equally viable.

4.2 A shortcut to a guaranteed solution

Some researchers have recommended a technique which will still lead to the guaranteed best answer without necessarily having to examine every one of the possible flowcharts. The original papers on this are by Reinwald and Soland[22] and readers who cannot be satisfied with anything less than a rigorous mathematical treatment of the technique are advised to consult those articles. I hope the following explanation of the method is an easier to read indication of the approach though possibly lacking conclusiveness.

For example take the following condition part of a decision table

	R1	R2	R3	R4	C	S
C1	Y	N	N	N	8	0
C2	–	Y	N	Y	8	4
C3	–	Y	–	N	8	6
	0·50	0·125	0·25	0·125	$\overline{24} - \overline{10} = 14$	
	A	B	C	D		

Assume that the criterion on which we wish to maximise is run time cost. The figure at the foot of each rule indicates the probability with which that rule will be used in relation to all rules. The first column, C, to the right of the table indicates the cost of obeying each condition in some unit which might be number of instructions, for instance. In this case each condition costs the same as any other. These, then, are all the assumptions in this case and now to proceed with the resolution.

Consider first the range in which our target lies. We can see that in no use of the table will we have to perform more than three tests. Another way of putting it is to say that applying all the possible cases once each to the worst flowchart will take no more than $3 \times 8 = 24$ instructions. On the other hand by judicious choosing of the sequence of the tests we can reduce some of the path-lengths. Suppose we leave condition 2 until the end of all the branches. Any case that identifies as rule 1 will not require condition 2 to be tested (the dash indicates that the answer is immaterial). The probability of rule 1 is 0·5. That is, half the cases at run time will not obey the eight instructions of the C2 test. The column to the right of the decision table labelled S shows for each condition the savings that could be made by leaving this condition until last. The figure 4 against C2 is the probability of rule 1, 0·5 multiplied by the cost of C1, 8.

Suppose instead we left condition 3 to the end of all the branches. The result of C3 is immaterial in any rule 1 case or any rule 3 case. The probability of missing the eight instructions of the C3 test is therefore $0·50 + 0·25 = 0·75$. $0·75$ of $8 = 6$ shown against C3 in column S. We save nothing by keeping C1 to the end and so its S entry is zero. Of course it is not possible to save every condition to the end, but if we could then the total saving would be $0 + 4 + 6 = 10$. And now we know our target. We cannot expect a flowchart which has an

35

average run cost which is better than 24 − 10 = 14. It was necessary to establish this as our search for the best flowchart can cease as soon as we find one with an average run cost of 14.

All the possible flowcharts can be regarded as belonging to three sets: those beginning with a test of C1, those beginning with C2, and those beginning with C3 (Fig. 4.3).

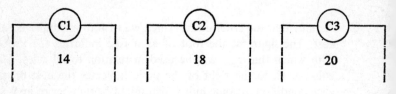

Fig. 4.3

We decided that if we could save C3 to the end then we would have a run cost saving of 6, so if we take C3 first we sacrifice a saving of 6 and we can say that all the flowcharts in that set cannot have a better run cost than 20. A similar argument establishes that within the set beginning with C2 we cannot have a better run cost than 18. Taking C1 first makes no sacrifice at all so the set beginning with test C1 might contain one with a run cost of 14. Note that we cannot say that the best one is in the set of those charts beginning C1; we can only say that that is the set worth further examination at the moment – we must not yet reject the others.

Having checked C1 and got a Yes, action A is called for without more ado but on the No side there is a sub-table like this

				S
C2	Y	N	Y	0
C3	Y	–	N	2
	0·25	0·5	0·25	

with its run cost savings. It is now possible to regard one of our three sets as breakable into two further sets, C1 No leading to C2, and C1 No leading to C3. The former of these makes no sacrifice in savings and the latter makes a sacrifice of 2 by not leaving C3 to the end.

36

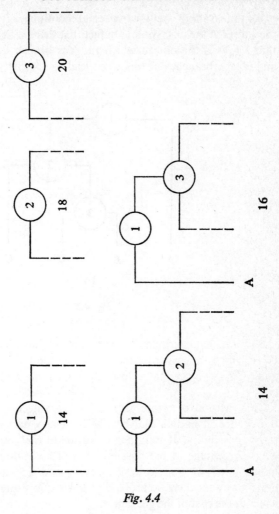

Fig. 4.4

It is the leftmost set, in Fig. 4.4, that looks the most interesting. But note that if the last developed two sets had shown that neither contained a possibility that was better than 19, then we should have continued our breakdown of the set beginning with test C2 because its best possibility of 18 would, in those circumstances, have looked the most interesting.

37

As things stand, however, we shall continue our exploration with the subset at the left. We find in fact that there is only one member of that set, it is the one in which the Yes branch of C2 leads to C3 and all the branches of this chart lead to specific actions (Fig. 4.5).

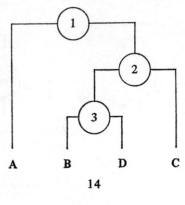

14

Fig. 4.5

So we have unearthed a flowchart which has an average run cost of 14 which we earlier established to be the best run cost available and we have no need to explore any of the remaining possibilities.

This method therefore gives us a guaranteed best solution with the chance of finding that best without necessarily exploring every single possibility. It is rather unfortunate that we cannot forecast what percentage of the possibilities will be examined and it could happen that we had to look at every one. In anything but small decision tables then we probably cannot afford the translation time which is the cost of the guarantee.

The example given aimed at minimum run-time cost, but the method can be adapted to give the best solution in terms of minimum storage.

5 A closer look at branch conversion

5.1 Limiting the examination

In order to keep within the realm of practical translation we must search for some strategy that avoids looking at so many of the possibilities. The cost of shortening translate time will be giving up the idea of getting the guaranteed best and settling for something that is just pretty good. Most of the published translation tactics are just that, but it is a shame that inventors of such tactics do not admit that they do not give certain bests and, what is more, do not explain why they are planning for the merely acceptable. Since we have conscientiously worked out how the very best can be judged and the difficulties about calculating it then we can, with a clean conscience, examine some short-term tactics.

The whole business is very much akin to the other fascinating problem of programming a chess player. The game of chess is a determinable game. That is to say there is a unique play for each player that represents the very best that he can do. To discover what it is we simply have to draw a large tree of chess boards, the board at the very top showing the opening position. Branches out of this are taken to boards at level two, one board depicting each of White's possible opening moves (there are twenty of them). Out of each of those we draw branches to more boards depicting all of Black's possible answers. We continue with further levels until we get to the ends of all the branches at checkmate or drawn situations. Having done that we might find, because of White's advantage of having the first move, that a set of moves is open to him such that however Black replies White can always move to victory. It might be, though it is very unlikely, that it is a disadvantage to go first and that Black can always force a win. The third possibility is that the tree will show that both sides can always reply to each other so as to prevent the other winning, and that means that a draw is inevitable if both players play the right moves. In fact only one of these three situations is the true fact about the game of chess and the reason no one can say for sure which is the actual case is that the number of boards in the tree that I described would be astronomical. There is no possibility of a computer ever being able to make the analysis. So chess-playing programs have to be content with various limited strategies. Most of them have a means of creating the boards down to several levels and this is combined with a formula for evaluating the boards at the ends of the branches. They vary in the evaluation formula and in the manner in which a selective examination of the game tree is conducted. The method we used for developing the tree of flow-charts is frequently used; that is of developing branches at each level out of only the most interesting nodes. The limited analysis was practical to a guaranteed best solution only in the case of the smaller decision tables we decided, but why should we not use some limited exploration techniques as in the chess problem so as to get, if not a guaranteed best one, then at least a pretty good one? What this means in practice is that we shall end up with a fairly economic flowchart, but will miss the equivalent of a brilliant queen sacrifice; that is a case where the choice of which condition to take next looks inappropriate at the time, but opens the field for later choices to be made with maximum economies.

Many of the techniques described in the literature on decision table translation concern themselves with tactics for choosing the condition to constitute the next test in the flowchart. The flowchart is developed node at a time and the tactic applied at each node. But this is somewhat unimaginative. It corresponds in the chess-playing program to selecting only the one best looking move out of each position. Every chess player knows that it cannot be a very good game in which each player looks only one move ahead, and our main idea in making the translation of decision tables automatic is not to save us manual work, but rather to get the job done better than we mere humans could expect to do it.

Nevertheless it is worthwhile studying some of these tactics because they suggest ways of limiting our development of the tree of flowcharts.

5.2 Establishing a convention

Each expert uses his own type of diagram and it will be difficult to compare the tactics unless we devise a common form of diagram, so let me join the experts in proposing a representation that can be consistent throughout this book. The aim is to slightly modify the appearance of a decision table so that it can be manipulated in a way that makes it clear what step has been taken and to end up with a modified decision table which maps obviously on to a flowchart. I am assuming that if the modification and the matching is obvious then any programmer so inclined can work up his own coding. The essential is that the reader can follow the development by just looking at the pictures as he reads straight through the text. I shall take the following decision table and make the necessary changes to produce an equivalent flowchart without regard to optimisation in the first instance.

```
C1   Y - N Y
C2   N Y N N
C3   Y - - N
     A B C D
```

It has already been made clear that swopping row for row in a decision table or swopping column for column makes no difference to the logic. In our series of transformations we shall not be disturbing the contents of any column (rule) but we shall be dealing with parts of rows. The first convention therefore is that instead of identifying the condition once by a number at the left-hand end of the row I shall attach the condition number to each Y or N or dash in the row like this

```
1Y 1- 1N 1Y
2N 2Y 2N 2N
3Y 3- 3- 3N
A  B  C  D
```

Having decided quite at random that I will test condition 2 first I shall move the row dealing with 2s to the top of the group.

```
2N 2Y 2N 2N
1Y 1–  1N 1Y
3Y 3–  3–  3N

A  B  C  D
```

And then all 2 elements that are Y I move to the left leaving all 2N type rules to the right. Like this

```
2Y 2N 2N 2N
1–  1Y 1N 1Y
3–  3Y 3–  3N

B  A  C  D
```

I now indicate that a test on condition 2 has been made by underlining this first row, and then by drawing a vertical between the first and second rule I indicate the two dependent decision sub-tables that hang on the branches of this first test.

```
2Y│2N 2N 2N
1–│1Y 1N 1Y
3–│3Y 3–  3N
 B│ A  C  D
```

Note the partial flowchart now determined. I have continued this convention that the left branch is the Yes branch and the right-hand one is the No branch. Because there is only one action, B, in the left-hand decision sub-table, I can infer that no more tests have to be made in that branch. In the right-hand decision sub-table my dice tells me to take condition 3 for the next test and so I swop two rows but only in the right-hand sub-table.

```
2Y│2N 2N 2N
1–│3Y 3–  3N
3–│1Y 1N 1Y
 B│ A  C  D
```

I would now expect to sort this sub-table so that all the Ys in the top row were together on the left, but one of the elements is 3–

so the rule in which this occurs must be expanded into two rules before I can make the split.

2Y	2N	2N	2N	2N
1–	3Y	3Y	3N	3N
3–	1Y	1N	1N	1Y
B	A	C	C	D

The toned area contains the two rules that have replaced the one. We note in passing that increasing the number of rules cannot be a good thing but let us continue to develop the chart.

2Y	2N	2N	2N	2N
1–	3Y	3Y	3N	3N
3–	1Y	1N	1N	1Y
B	A	C	C	D

The action row is now broken in three. The first part contains action B only and needs no further resolution, indeed it might make the table clearer if I now leave out the insignificant elements in the first column, namely the 1– and 3–. The next table shows a further test differentiating between actions A and C.

2Y	2N	2N	2N	2N
	3Y	3Y	3N	3N
	1Y	1N	1N	1Y
B	A	C	C	D

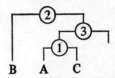

Only one small sub-table remains unresolved, that leading to actions C and D and I shall swop the cells to get the Y on the left and then complete the breakdown.

2Y	2N	2N	2N	2N
	3Y	3Y	3N	3N
	1Y	1N	1Y	1N
B	A	C	D	C

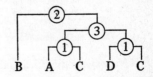

43

In essence what we have been doing is to swop columns and rows of the tables until we have broken it into sections. Each section contains insignificant dashes or terms which are the same, and each section at the foot of the table contains separate actions. If in those sections containing similar elements I exclude all but one identifying element you will easily be able to map the modified table on to the flowchart.

5.3 Varying 'next condition'

So much for the mechanism we shall use for illustrating the development of flowcharts from decision tables. Now let us concentrate on the effects of choosing different conditions when we come to 'next test'. Here is the same starting decision table.

```
C1   Y – N Y
C2   N Y N N
C3   Y – – N
     A B C D
```

Last time we started with condition 2, and since there were no dashes in that row no expansion of the rule columns was necessary. But suppose we had chosen condition 1 first, then because condition 1 has a dash in the rule that leads to action B then we should have had to increase the number of rules immediately.

```
1Y  1Y 1N  1N 1Y
2N  2Y 2Y  2N 2N
3Y  3–  3–  3– 3N
 A   B  B   C  D
```

Now swop the third and fifth columns to get the Ys to the left,

```
1Y 1Y 1Y│1N 1N              ┌──①──┐
2N 2Y 2N│2N 2Y
3Y 3─ 3N│3─ 3─
 A  B  D│ C  B
```

Two sub-tables both need resolution. Consider the right-hand one leading to C and B; if we take condition 2 as the next test there, a simple left-right swop precedes the next breakdown, but suppose we had decided to test condition 3 first.

```
      1Y│1N                 ┌──①──┐
2N 2Y 2N│3─ 3─
3Y 3─ 3N│2N 2Y
 A  B  D│ C  B
```

Floating row 3 in the right-hand part above 2 gives us two dash rules to expand before we can do the next breakdown. The next picture expands and sorts the Ys from the Ns in one step.

```
   1Y│1N                    ┌──①──┐
2N 2Y 2N│3Y 3Y│3N 3N              ┌──③──┐
3Y 3─ 3N│2N 2Y│2N 2Y
 A  B  D│ C  B│ C  B
```

Clearly the branches from test 3 will each require a test of 2. Suppose that in the left-hand sub-table I decide again foolishly to take test 3 first then I shall have to double up the 3─ that leads to action B. The completed resolution along these lines comes out as follows

```
         1Y│1N                        ┌────────①────────┐
   3Y │3N │   3Y │3N           ┌──③──┐         ┌──③──┐
2Y│2N│2Y│2N│2Y│2N│2Y│2N      ┌②┐   ┌②┐       ┌②┐   ┌②┐
B │A │B │D │B │C │B │C        B   A B   D   B   C B   C
```

From this experience we can draw the conclusion that to take too early a condition which has dashes in its row leads to expansion and increases the number of tests in the flowchart. Taking first a condition that has no dashes avoids expansion on that step and also, as in the first of the two resolutions, avoids a need to deal with some of the other dashes that come later. Now you are familiar with the representation of the breakdown we shall in the next chapter investigate some useful tactics for choosing the sequence of tests.

6 Tactics to determine next test

6.1 Dash count

A simple rule for next condition selection might be 'count the dashes in each row and choose the one with the lowest dash count' (see Pollock [20]). However, look at the following decision table.

```
1  - - N N Y   2
2  N Y Y N -   1
3  Y Y Y Y -   1
4  Y Y - - N   2
5  N Y N Y -   1
   A B C D E
```

If we were guided by the simple dash count then conditions 2, 3 and 5 look the best bets. The expansion of the dash in condition 2, rule E, however puts the dash of condition 3, rule E, into both sub-tables. Furthermore when we come to expand each of those we might be putting copies of the dash of condition 4, rule E, into each sub-table of each of those sub-tables. When considering each dash we must give a thought therefore to how many other dashes there are in the same column or how many may be generated. We observed earlier that in a limited entry table n dashes in a rule meant that the rule was an abbreviation for 2^n specific rules. The following decision table is the same one as above.

```
1  - - N N Y   4
2  N Y Y N -   8
3  Y Y Y Y -   8
4  Y Y - - N   4
5  N Y N Y -   8
   A B C D E
   2 2 2 2 8   rules represented
```

The numbers below each rule indicate the number of real rules represented by that column. The number at the right of each condition is calculated by adding the dashes but, instead of counting one for each dash, counting the number at the foot of the column in which that dash occurs.

Let us now break down this table into a flowchart in two different ways: first using the rule that for each sub-table we take the condition to test next as the one with the minimum number of dashes, and second using the rule that for each sub-table we take the condition to test next as the one with the minimum *weighted* dash count.

All rows have dashes but 2, 3 and 5 have only one each so take condition 2 first.

```
2Y 2Y 2Y│2N 2N 2N          ┌─②─┐
1─ 1N 1Y│1─ 1N 1Y
3Y 3Y 3─│3Y 3Y 3─
4Y 4─ 4N│4Y 4─ 4N
5Y 5N 5─│5N 5Y 5─
 B  C  E│ A  D  E
```

Each of the conditions in each of the sub-tables has one dash so the choice is immaterial. I am taking conditions 3 next in both. (Now that you are getting used to the mechanics I shall start interchanging rows and shifting the Ys of the major row to the left in one operation.)

```
          2Y│2N
3Y 3Y 3Y│3N│3Y 3Y 3Y│3N              ┌──②──┐
1─ 1N 1Y│1Y│1─ 1N 1Y│1Y        ┌─③─┐      ┌─③─┐
4Y 4─ 4N│4N│4Y 4─ 4N│4N
5Y 5N 5─│5─│5N 5Y 5─│5─
 B  C  E│ E│ A  D  E│ E          E          E
```

There are now four sub-tables but two of them have resolved to action E. Each row of each of the two remaining sub-tables has one dash and I am going to take condition 5 next in both cases.

48

	2Y		2N	
	3Y	3N	3Y	3N
5Y 5Y	5N 5N		5Y 5Y	5N 5N
1— 1Y	1Y 1N		1Y 1N	1— 1Y
4Y 4N	4N 4—		4N 4—	4Y 4N
B E	E C	E	E D	A E E

(tree diagram: 2 — 3 — 5 — E, E ; 3 — 5 — E, E)

Now there are six sub-tables including the two that have resolved to action E already. In the leftmost sub-table condition 4 has no dashes and a test of it distinguishes between action B and E. In the next sub-table a test on 1 distinguishes between E and C. The remaining two have no dashes in 1 and 4, respectively, and testing these completes the resolution using minimum dash count as the rule.

	2Y		2N	
	3Y	3N	3Y	3N
	5Y	5N	5Y	5N
4Y	4N 1Y 1N		1Y 1N 4Y	4N
1—	1Y 4N 4—		4N 4— 1—	1Y
B	E E C	E	E D A	E E

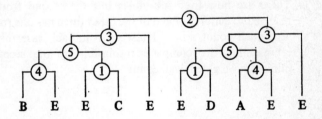

Now to perform the second resolution on the same table using the minimum *weighted* dash count tactic. This gives us a choice of conditions 1 or 4 as first choice – each has a weighted dash count (WDC) of 4. Take 1 first.

W D C

1Y	1Y	1Y	1N	1N	1N	1N	4
2N	2Y	2–	2N	2Y	2Y	2N	8
3Y	3Y	3–	3Y	3Y	3Y	3Y	8
4Y	4Y	3N	4Y	4Y	4–	4–	4
5N	5Y	5–	5N	5Y	5N	5Y	8
A	B	E	A	B	C	D	

```
        ┌──(1)──┐
```

The left-hand sub-table has no dashes in condition 4 so that is decisive. The right-hand sub-table has no dashes in 2, 3 and 5 and I shall take 2 next.

		1Y	1N			
4Y	4Y	4N	2Y	2Y	2N	2N
2N	2Y	2–	3Y	3Y	3Y	3Y
3Y	3Y	3–	3Y	4–	4–	4Y
5N	5Y	5–	5Y	5N	5Y	5N
A	B	E	B	C	D	A

```
      ┌──(1)──┐
    (4)       (2)
```

There are now four sub-tables but the second from the left has resolved to action E. Each of the other three has one row at least with zero dash count and if I test on 5 in each case this is the result representing the complete resolution by the second method – minimum weighted dash count.

	1Y	1N				
4Y	4N	·	2Y	2N		
5Y	5N	·	5Y	5N	5Y	5N
2Y	2N	·	3Y	3Y	3Y	3Y
3Y	3Y	·	4Y	4–	4–	4Y
B	A	E	B	C	D	A

```
              ┌────────(1)────────┐
         ┌──(4)──┐           ┌──(2)──┐
       (5)                 (5)       (5)
        │   │   │   │    │    │   │
        B   A   E   B    C    D   A
```

Now compare the two results. Here are the two flowcharts

By Simple Dash Count (SDC)

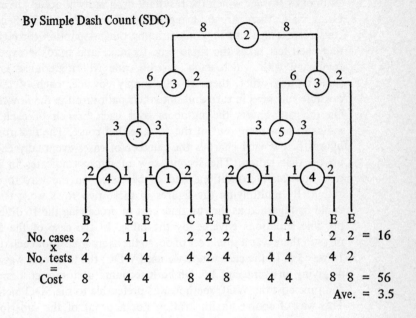

	B	E	E		C	E	E	D	A		E	E	
No. cases	2	1	1		2	2	2	1	1		2	2	= 16
x													
No. tests	4	4	4		4	2	4	4	4		4	2	
=													
Cost	8	4	4		8	4	8	4	4		8	8	= 56

Ave. = 3.5

By Weighted Dash Count (WDC)

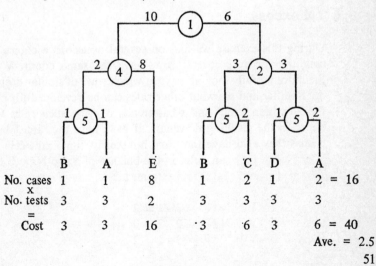

	B	A	E	B	C	D	A	
No. cases	1	1	8	1	2	1	2	= 16
x								
No. tests	3	3	2	3	3	3	3	
=								
Cost	3	3	16	·3	·6	3	6	= 40

Ave. = 2.5

51

First, notice the actual number of tests which is indicative of the amount of storage which the resultant program will occupy in store. Using SDC there are 9, using WDC there are only 6. Second, consider average run time. Continuing our assumption throughout that each test takes the same time to make and that the expected frequency with which each possible rule will materialise is the same as any other, then we can simply consider each of the 16 possible rule keys in turn and note their path through the flowchart. On the two charts the numbers over each branch of each test indicates how many out of the 16 take that route. The first row of figures below each chart is the number of cases eventually ending up on that action. The second row of figures indicates in each case how many conditions had to be tested on the way to each action. By multiplying the figures in these two rows we get what could be regarded as the run time cost of processing the 16 different possible situations covered by the table. In the case of the SDC method there was a total cost of 56, so the average cost for each of the 16 was 3·5. In the case where we used WDC, the total cost was only 40 giving an average of 2·5. On both accounts (a) storage cost and (b) run time cost the WDC method was preferable to the SDC method. This was of course an illustration not a proof of the superiority, but you can easily convince yourself with examples of your own.

6.2 YN excess

During this exercise we had on several occasions a choice of next condition because several rows gave the same count. We could therefore usefully look at ways in which rows of similar dash counts might differ and see what other rules can be developed for choosing the 'next condition' and what trends obeying such rules are produced in the resulting flowchart. If rows have the same number of dashes they also have the same number of significant cells, that is Y or N, but they can differ in the balance of Ys to Ns (see Press[21]). This next example takes two extreme tables.

$$1 \quad Y N N N \quad 3-1=2$$
$$2 \quad Y Y N N \quad 2-2=0$$
$$3 \quad Y Y Y N \quad 3-1=2$$

Against each condition row there is a little sum in which the operands are the totals of the Ns and the Ys and in which the smaller is subtracted from the larger to give what we could call the YN excess. If we choose to take as the next condition in our resolution the row with the maximum YN excess then we have the option of 1 or 3 for first choice. This diagram supposes 1.

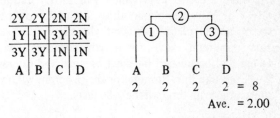

1Y	1N	1N	1N
2Y	2Y	2N	2N
3Y	3Y	3Y	3N
A	B	C	D

A   B   C   D
1   2   3   3 = 9

Ave. = 2.25

After the first chop the part-row 2 had two Ns and one Y whilst the part-3 row had two Ys and one N so there was an option 2 or 3 for the second chop; in either case the shape of the flowchart is the same. Note that it is a very biased chart. A mobile constructed this way would need A to be heavier than B which should be heavier than C, etc.

On the other hand if we used as a method of selecting next condition test the *minimum* YN excess then the resolution would have gone like this.

2Y	2Y	2N	2N
1Y	1N	3Y	3N
3Y	3Y	1N	1N
A	B	C	D

A   B   C   D
2   2   2   2 = 8

Ave. = 2.00

Note that this chart is a balanced one, and with A B C D all equal in weight we would have a satisfactory mobile. The given decision table had four possible keys each of which would take a separate route through to its particular action. The digits below each action letter in the two preceding charts give the number of tests that would be made before reaching that action. Adding these and dividing by four gives what could be regarded as an average cost (in unit tests) of processing these keys at run time. Note particularly that the balanced chart gives the better average run time cost. The amount of storage required was the same in both cases – that is three tests.

Algorithms in the literature using the YN excess factor often propose using minimum YN excess if the criterion for best is short run time. Maximum YN excess is proposed where the criterion is least storage. It is fairly certain that the former is true but there is doubt about the latter, neither Press[21] nor Pollock[20] gives examples of the balanced chart taking more storage than the biased one and such examples are difficult to find. Much depends of course on the other rules making up any particular algorithm. Take the following case in which the YN factor is the only one considered.

		SE	WE
1	Y Y Y N N N	$3 - 3 = 0$	$4 - 3 = 1$
2	Y N N N N N	$5 - 1 = 4$	$6 - 1 = 5$
3	N N N Y – N	$4 - 1 = 3$	$5 - 2 = 3$
4	N Y N N Y N	$4 - 2 = 2$	$4 - 3 = 1$
5	N N N N Y N	$5 - 1 = 4$	$5 - 2 = 3$
	A B C D E F		

The table labelled SE gives the calculation of the simple excess. The other table labelled WE gives a weighted excess – that is to say, recognition has been given to the fact that, because of the dash at 3E there are two keys which will satisfy action E and therefore any Y or N in the column above E should count twice when adding the Ys and Ns; let us play first with the simple excess. Going for the rule 'minimum excess for a balanced chart', condition 1 will be tested first because of its exact balance and the rest of the table will work out like this. Storage for the program will include six tests and the average run time will be 2·86 tests.

1Y	1Y	1Y	1N	1N	1N	1N
2Y	2N	2N	3Y	3Y	3N	3N
4N	4Y	4N	5Y	5N	4Y	4N
3N	3N	3N	4Y	4N	5Y	5N
5N	5N	5N	2N	2N	2N	2N
A	B	C	E	D	E	F

A	B	C	E	D	E	F	
2	3	3	3	3	3	3	= 20

Ave. = 2.8

Now again using the simple excess we will aim at the biased chart through maximum YN excess. The SE table offers us two candidates, conditions 2 and 5 both with an excess of four. Here is the resolution taking 5 first.

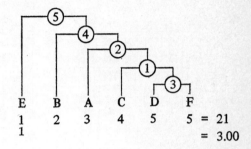

5Y	5N	5N	5N	5N	5N
4Y	4Y	4N	4N	4N	4N
2N	2N	2Y	2N	2N	2N
1N	1Y	1Y	1Y	1N	1N
3–	3N	3N	3N	3Y	3N
E	B	A	C	D	F

```
E    B    A    C    D    F
1    2    3    4    5    5  = 21
1                          = 3.00
```

Storage will include five tests as against the six tests of the balanced chart but the average run time will be greater – 3·00 as against 2·86. Although the balanced chart seems to take more store, in the balanced case after the first chop in the right-hand sector we took condition 3 with two Ys and two Ns as next candidate, but we might have taken either a test on 5 or 4 because they too had two Ys and two Ns. Had we done so we would have had a flowchart of only 5 tests – no worse than the biased chart.

Now to see how things work out using the weighted excess instead of the simple one. Again we will compare the balanced with the biased objective. This time both rules 1 and 4 offer a minimum excess of 1 so let's take 4 for a change. Here is the resolution

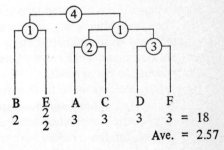

4Y	4Y	4N	4N	4N	4N
1Y	1N	1Y	1Y	1N	1N
2N	2N	2Y	2N	3Y	3N
3N	3–	3N	3N	2N	2N
5N	5Y	5N	5N	5N	5N
B	E	A	C	D	F

```
B    E    A    C    D    F
2    2    3    3    3    3  = 18
     2
       Ave. = 2.57
```

Note only five tests and an average of 2·57 for an object run. There is a single candidate for the biased approach – condition 2 with a weighted YN excess of 5. Remember, though, that this was an alternative when we were using SE.

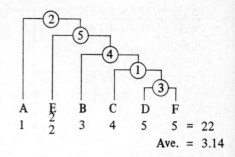

2Y	2N	2N	2N	2N	2N
5N	5Y	5N	5N	5N	5N
4N	4Y	4Y	4N	4N	4N
1Y	1N	1Y	1Y	1N	1N
3N	3–	3N	3N	3Y	3N
A	E	B	C	D	F

```
         A    E    B    C    D    F
         1    2    3    4    5    5  = 22
              2
                              Ave. = 3·14
```

The storage cost of five tests is the same but notice that although the shape of the chart is similar to the biased chart beginning with test condition 5, the average run time has increased from 3·00 to 3·14. This is because there are two keys leading to action E (the dash in condition 3 row). When we took 5 first both of these keys are sorted out on the first test. When we took 2 first these two keys took two tests to resolve.

These examples I hope have given a familiarity with experimenting with various tactics and combinations of tactics. They have also shown how unreasonable it is to be dogmatic about the superiority of one method over another. Very frequently the algorithm leads to equality of candidates where the choice is arbitrary but the results are vitally different. Whatever algorithms are devised which do not explore all the possibilities (or at least all the possibilities necessary to reach a precalculated target) can only be regarded as good tries. They may achieve the optimum in a large number of cases. They may give near optimal solutions in many other cases but there will always remain some cases where some other algorithm would have produced a better result.

However, we have to face up to the fact that the methods for guaranteed optimal solutions are too expensive of translation time to be useful for practical sized decision tables and that we must be content for the moment with decision table processors which use algorithms involving tactics such as we have just been examining based on comparisons of the attributes of one row against another. Without therefore being categorical let us in summary observe some tendencies.

6.3 Summarising on short tactics

The positioning of the dashes is probably the most critical factor and the YN excess is a secondary consideration. Counts of dashes, Ys and Ns can with some advantage be weighted by considering the actual number of rules represented by each column of the decision table. The difficulty here is that this takes into account factors which may not materially affect the outcome once we start resolving into sub-tables. A method aimed at a biased chart will fairly certainly give storage economy but there is a high risk of the average run time being greater than in the more balanced chart. Aiming at the balanced chart will almost certainly give the best run time average but the risk of that being at the cost of storage is low.

These conclusions are made ignoring the facts that the tests may vary in the time it takes to make them and that the occurrences of the keys may vary in frequency. A program created from a decision table may appear to give good behaviour for some time and then may deteriorate as the pattern of the data changes from week to week. Later we must see whether we can cater for varying condition cost and rule frequency.

7 Compromise methods

In producing flowcharts from decision tables we have looked at what might first appear to be two different approaches. In Chapter 4 we discussed the possibility of producing all the possible flowcharts from a given decision table and then measuring to find the best according to the given criteria. We then looked at a modification to this method in which we first calculated a target figure. By proceeding carefully with the development of all the flowcharts, so that we opened up the tree along the branch which looked most likely to lead to the target, we opened up the possibility of achieving a

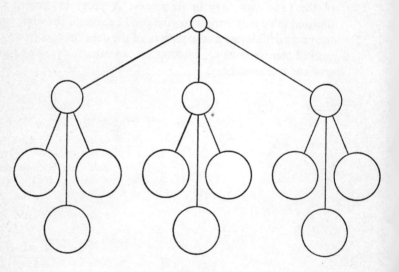

Fig. 7.1

flowchart which we knew to be the optimum before we had necessarily developed every one. Even so this method was impractically
long on sizeable decision tables.

Then in Chapter 6 we examined a number of tactics which could
be combined in various ways to give algorithms all aimed at deciding
which single condition to test next in the branches of the developing
flowchart. These methods are in fact only tightly limited versions of
the first kind of Chapter 4. In Figs. 7.1 and 7.2 the circles represent
the developing flowcharts – getting larger at each level. Fig. 7.1
represents the exhaustive approach. Fig. 7.2 represents the 'quick
tactic' approach in which at each level we look at the next possible
conditions and just select one from which the development is to
continue.

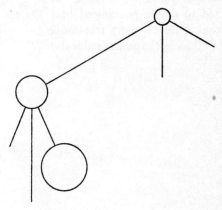

Fig. 7.2

Now between these two extremes there must be several useful
compromises and this is currently an unexplored area in which a
detailed investigation is badly needed. The following list indicates a
few of the lines that might be followed for a compromise solution.

1. Use the exhaustive method up to a preset level. Take the best
chart at that level and then develop it by one of the 'quick tactic'
methods.

2. Use the exhaustive method for a fixed period of time and then
use the quick tactics to continue from the best chart found in the set
time.

3.　At each level of the tree in turn develop all the possible flow-charts but at each level abandon all but the most interesting 2 or 3 charts for developing to the next level.

4.　In the modified exhaustive method we calculated a target cost which told us when we had got a flowchart which could not be improved upon. One could proceed as in the exhaustive method but transfer to the single choice tactics as soon as the developing charts had approached say 75 per cent of the way to the target.

5.　Decide a size of table upon which it is practical to operate the exhaustive method. Use the quick tactics until the sub-tables produced at the ends of the charts are that size.

Unlike the exhaustive method, none of these methods can be expected to give a guaranteed best. On the other hand they will in exchange for the extra translation time give a more satisfactory solution than by the quick tactics alone.

8 Some other factors

8.1 The tactics related to extended numeric

All the examples given so far have dealt with limited entry decision tables and although I pointed out earlier that these were only a particular case of the numeric extended table we could usefully investigate how the tactics we have been examining might equally apply to the extended case.

First consider completeness in an extended numeric. The total number of possible rules is given by the product of the numbers which for each row represents the number of possible states. Here again is the complete picture for a three-condition table in which the number of possibilities is 3, 2 and 4, respectively. The possible number of rules is $3 \times 2 \times 4 = 24$.

```
C1   1 1 1 1 1 1 1 1 2 2 2 2 2 2 2 2 3 3 3 3 3 3 3 3
C2   1 1 1 1 2 2 2 2 1 1 1 1 2 2 2 2 1 1 1 1 2 2 2 2
C3   1 2 3 4 1 2 3 4 1 2 3 4 1 2 3 4 1 2 3 4 1 2 3 4
```

If in such a table dashes are used for abbreviation then any one dash indicates that so many rules have been amalgamated. How many is given by the number of possible states of the condition in which row the dash occurs. For example

```
C1   3
C2   2
C3   –
```

represents 4 rules because there are 4 possible outcomes of C3. The above column, in fact, covers the last four columns in the complete table above it. A rule with several dashes in it will represent the number of rules you get by multiplying together the number of

61

possibilities for which each dash stands. For example

C1	–	(3 possibilities)
C2	2	(2 possibilities)
C3	–	(4 possibilities)

represent $3 \times 4 = 12$ rules. Here is a more elaborate example in which is shown at the foot of each column the number of rules represented. Since we know that the total number of possible rules is $4 \times 2 \times 3 = 24$ we can assess that the decision table is a complete one and by using the numbers along the bottom we can calculate a weighted dash count for each column if we are adopting resolution tactics based on that factor.

```
                                        WDC
C1   1 2 – 1 4 4 2 3 4 1 3 1 1 2 3 3     4
C2   2 1 1 2 1 2 1 2 1 2 – 1 1 2 2 1     2
C3   1 3 1 2 3 – 3 1 2 3 2 3 2 – 3 3     6
     . . . . . . . . . . . . . . . .
     1 1 4 1 1 3 1 1 1 1 2 1 1 3 1 1—→24
```

When discussing limited entry tables we investigated the differences in aiming at biased or balanced flow diagrams. We can do this with numeric extended tables as well. To help us here, though, we shall construct another table so that we can see what question to ask next. (The method was proposed by Montalbano[17] who uses some very good diagrams.) Take for instance this decision table (not a complete one).

```
                               1 2 3 4
C1 1 1 1 1 2 2 2 3            ④3 1
C2 1 1 2 4 1 1 3 2           ④2 1 1
C3 1 2 1 2 3 4 1 2            3 3 1 1
   A B C D E F G H
```

The little table to the right indicates under each digit the number of times that that digit occurs along the line. If we are aiming at a balanced chart then we argue that there are eight digits in each line. Half the possibilities can be picked out by asking the question 'does C1 = 1'. Asking 'does C2 = 1' would be equally effective in giving two sub-tables of equal size. For each of the sub-tables we should draw the little frequency table and each time ask which breaks the table into two equal parts or as near equal as possible. The result of all this can be indicated by Fig. 8.1 in a form with which you should now be familiar.

C1	1	1	1	1	2	2	2	3
C2	1	1	2	4	1	1	3	2
C3	1	2	1	2	3	4	1	2
	A	B	C	D	E	F	G	H

Fig. 8.1

If on the other hand we are aiming at a biased chart we will need the frequency table again but this time to see where there is the least, ideally one, occurrence of a digit in any row. In such a case with one question we can isolate a rule.

```
                        1 2 3 4
    C1 1 1 1 1 2 2 2 3    4 3 ①
    C2 1 1 2 4 1 1 3 2    4 2 ① ①
    C3 1 2 1 2 3 4 1 2    3 3 ① ①
       A B C D E F G H
```

There are five different questions we could ask to distinguish a rule namely 'does C1 = 3', 'does C2 = 3', does C2 = 4', does C3 = 3', 'does C3 = 4'. If we produce a string of tests in that order we shall isolate rules H G D E F in that order. The remaining sub-table and its frequency table look like this.

```
                    1 2
    C1 1 1 1        3 —
    C2 1 1 2        2 ①
    C3 1 2 1        2 ①
       A B C
```

A test 'does C2 = 2' with the answer 'yes' leads to C and it remains only to distinguish between A and B. The resultant flowchart is as follows.

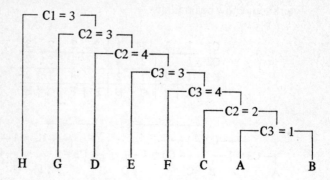

8.2 Other considerations

In all our examinations up to now we have for simplicity ignored certain factors, namely

(1) the storage occupied by the program steps which perform the tests,
(2) the different obey times of the instructions which constitute the tests,
(3) The various probabilities with which in real life the various rules are found appropriate.

Ignoring them has really meant that our conclusions have been reasonable only in the situations

(a) the storage occuped by every condition test is the same as for any other,
(b) every test takes the same time to resolve as any other.

On probability I have been guilty of inconsistency, sometimes assuming that all possible rules had the same probability and sometimes that all possible different outcomes (in terms of actions to be performed) had the same probability.

It will only be if we are vitally concerned with computer storage that factor (1) is of importance, so let us dismiss that one first. Recall the flowcharts that corresponded to a complete decision table of three conditions. They all have the same form – that is three levels of test; one opening to two at level two, opening to four at level three. They differed only in the order in which the tests were made. There were twelve possible sequences and on our earlier assumptions it looked as though there was nothing much to choose between them. But now let us assume that condition 1 takes many more instructions to resolve than condition 2 which in turn takes more instructions than condition 3. In Fig. 8.2 are two equivalent flowcharts for the same decision table but I have made the length of each block representing a test proportional to the number of machine instructions it contains. Thus you can measure the storage occupied by the whole tree of tests by adding together the lengths of the blocks.

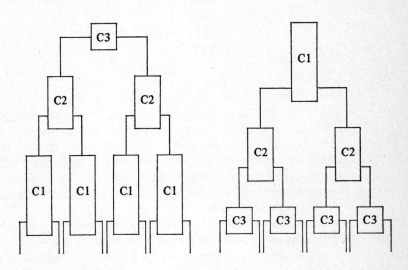

Fig. 8.2

Clearly they are very different in storage requirement. You may also recall the masking method of decision table resolution which entailed performing each test once and forming a profile of the answers which was then mapped on to each rule until a match was obtained. A similar representation of this method would be as in Fig. 8.3 but some additional storage would be required for the housekeeping task of forming the profile masking and matching. In all

65

it might prove a little more expensive than the tree beginning C1 but it would probably be more economic in storage than the tree beginning C3;

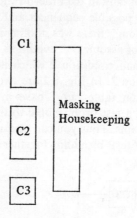

Fig. 8.3

One approach to the problem would be to generate a program which evaluated each condition and then, instead of creating the mask, to create a tree of tests. Because each test is a simple one – it has only to examine a previously calculated result – then the repetition of some of the tests would not bother us so much. By doing this we would lose the advantage that the tree method gives us, that on occasions when the table is incomplete or contains dashes all the conditions are not obeyed.

An alternative is to adopt the practice common in programming of creating subroutines for groups of instructions that would otherwise take up storage repeatedly. By making a subroutine of each condition test we have to store those instructions once only and the structure of the tree of tests is straightforward. It seems to me that such a tactic practically nullifies the advantage claimed for rule masking of minimising storage. Protagonists of the rule masking technique are also developing enhancement to the method which avoid the run time resolution of all the tests, so hopefully the existence of two completely separate, even antagonistic, schools of thought is disappearing.

9 The effects of rule frequency

9.1 Frequency and rule masking

The other two factors, cost of obeying a test and frequency of meeting the various rules in real life are much more interesting. In the standard rule masking technique, since we have to make each test once in every real case then the relative condition cost is irrelevant. In any developments of the technique in which it is possible to avoid some of the tests, the expensive ones are going to be those to avoid where possible.

In obeying programs produced by the rule masking technique the final part of the process is to map a pattern, rule by rule, until a match is found. The obey time will vary according to how many checks have to be made before a successful match. In arranging the sequence of rules, therefore, it will pay to put the most likely ones first. In Table 9.1 if the probability of any rule was the same as any other then the average number of checks in a sizeable number of real cases would be 4·5. If, however, the probabilities differed, as shown (the probabilities are shown as percentages), then the average number of checks would be 6·1 without sorting or 2·49 if suitably resequenced.

Table 9.1

Rule No.	1	2	3	4	5	6	7	8
No. of comparisons (8 cases)	1 +	2 +	3 +	4 +	5 +	6 +	7 +	8
							= 36 Ave 4·5	
New probability %	2	1	2	5	30	10	30	20
No. of comparisons (100 cases)	2 +	2 +	6 +	20 +	150 +	60 +	210 +	160
							= 610 Ave 6·1	
Rules resorted	5	7	8	6	4	1	3	2
Probability %	30	30	20	10	5	2	2	1
No. of comparisons	30 +	60 +	60 +	40 +	25 +	12 +	14 +	8
							= 249 Ave 2·4	

F

9.2 Frequency and branching

Consideration of the effect of frequency and run time cost is not quite so simple in respect of the branching technique. The following decision table can be analysed to produce either a biased chart as in AA or a balanced chart as in BB.

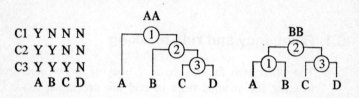

```
C1 Y N N N
C2 Y Y N N
C3 Y Y Y N
   A B C D
```

In each case the number of paths through the tree corresponds to the number of outcomes, namely four. If we suppose that each test costs 30 time units and the probability of the four outcomes is as shown in Table 9.2, then by multiplying one by the other we get a cost figure for each route. The total of the products is the run time cost for a hundred typical cases. Table 9.2 gives the statistics for chart AA.

Table 9.2

AA	Outcome	A	B	C	D
	Probability %	70	14	14	2
	Cost of tests (*each route*)	30	60	90	90
	Cost of tests (*100 cases*)	2100 + 840 + 1260 + 180 = 4380 Ave 43·8			

Table 9.3 gives similar statistics for chart BB.

Table 9.3

BB	Outcome	A	B	C	D
	Probability %	70	14	14	2
	Cost of tests (*each route*)	60	60	60	60
	Cost of tests (*100 cases*)	4200 + 840 + 840 + 120 = 6000 Ave 60·0			

Before we took into account condition cost and probability we came to the conclusion that the balanced chart would probably give the best average run time in practice. If, however, there is going to be a much greater popularity for route A then as the statistics show the biased chart AA turns out to be the better one.

Now let us make a different assumption about frequency, though again we assume each test costs 30 time units. Table 9.4 shows an evaluation in respect of charts AA and BB. In this instance notice that the average run time cost in the case of the balanced chart is better than the average run time cost for the biased chart.

Table 9.4

AA	Outcome	A	B	C	D
	Probability %	5	5	10	80
	Cost of tests (each route)	30	60	90	90
	Cost of tests (100 cases)	150 + 300 + 900 + 7200 = 8550 Ave 85·50			

BB	Outcome	A	B	C	D
	Probability %	5	5	10	80
	Cost of tests (each route)	60	60	60	60
	Cost of tests (100 cases)	300 + 300 + 600 + 4800 = 6000 Ave 60·00			

It is moreover interesting to note that if the previously assumed frequencies and costs hold then there is a third flowchart, still logically equivalent to the same decision table which gives an even better run time cost (Table 9.5).

Table 9.5

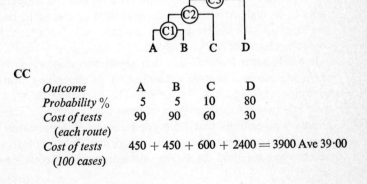

CC	Outcome	A	B	C	D
	Probability %	5	5	10	80
	Cost of tests (each route)	90	90	60	30
	Cost of tests (100 cases)	450 + 450 + 600 + 2400 = 3900 Ave 39·00			

The popularity rating for the given probabilities is then CC = 39·00, BB = 60·00, AA = 85·50.

9.3 Condition cost

Now whilst keeping the probabilities as in the last example let us suppose that the conditions have different resolution costs, namely

condition 1	2 time units,
condition 2	10 time units,
condition 3	100 time units.

Now a new evaluation of the three charts gives the results in Table 9.6.

Table 9.6

Outcome	A	B	C	D	
Probability	5	5	10	80	
AA route cost	2	12	112	112	
AA total cost (*100 cases*)	10 +	60 +	1120 +	8960 =	10150 Ave 101·50
BB route cost	12	12	110	110	
BB total cost (*100 cases*)	60 +	60 +	1100 +	8800 =	10020 Ave 100·20
CC route cost	112	112	110	100	
CC total cost (*100 cases*)	560 +	560 +	1100 +	8000 =	10220 Ave 102·20

This time the actual popularity rating has changed altogether: BB = 100·20, AA = 101·50, CC = 102·20, but the difference is so small as to make it seem that there is little to choose in respect of run time, and the choice between the three may have to be revised when the pattern of real data changes.

It would seem from all this that algorithms that we have earlier examined can lead to widely differing results depending on run time condition cost and rule frequency. The overall result is, I think, that if there is a wide divergence of these two factors then some short and easy algorithms that were good enough in most cases will be good enough in fewer cases. In the algorithms that took into account one row but weighted the findings according to what could be seen in the other rows we may find that some of those weightings are over compensatory. Variations in these factors put more and more emphasis on the use of methods which give a guaranteed best.

9.4 Taking frequency and cost into account

Nevertheless it is only fair to show how we can take test cost and frequency into account both in the dash count tactics and in the YN excess tactics. A nice adaptation of Pollock's algorithm, taking account of probability and using information theory, is given by Shweyder.[25]

I shall use again the same decision table as I used earlier to investigate methods based on simple and weighted dash count.

		Cost	Costed DC	SDC	WDC
C1	– – N N Y	7	315	2	4
C2	N Y Y N –	5	25	1	8
C3	Y Y Y Y –	6	20	1	8
C4	Y Y – – N	9	450	2	4
C5	N Y N Y –	3	15	1	8

Prob % 30 15 40 10 5

A B C D E

The figures in the first column after the table indicate supposed relative costs (they might be microseconds or instructions) of resolving the conditions. Condition 4 at 9 is the most expensive and condition 5 at 3 is the cheapest. The first row of figures below the table indicates the relative probabilities of the rules given as percentages. That is, out of a typical 100 cases, 30 will lead to action A, 15 to action B etc. Now let us weight the dashes in a different manner. In the rule that leads to A there is a dash against condition 1. The probability for rule A is 30 and the cost of condition 1 is 7 so the dash is worth $30 \times 7 = 210$. Similarly the dash in rule B condition 1 is worth $15 \times 7 = 105$. We can say that condition 1 has a costed dash count of $210 + 105 = 315$. Costing our dashes in this way gives the values shown in the second column to the right of the table. The minimum costed dash count is that of condition 5 with value 15. This was one of three possibilities using simple dash count and was neither of the two possibilities given by weighted dash count.

Now transpose the decision table to branch on condition 5 first.

		5Y	5Y	5Y	5N	5N	5N	
105	1–	1N	1Y	1–	1N	1Y	210
10	2Y	2N	2–	2N	2Y	2–	15
12	3Y	3Y	3–	3Y	3Y	3–	18
90	4Y	4–	4N	4Y	4–	4N	360
	B	D	E	A	C	E	
Prob % 15	10		2	30	40	3	

At either side of the sub-tables I have shown the new costed dash counts and these indicate that condition 2 is the preferred next test in both sub-tables. An awkward point was a necessity to provide a rule leading to action E in both sub-tables and we had only a single probability. This arose because we gave a probability for each outcome instead of anticipating the various routes through the ultimate chart. We ought to have expanded the decision table with dashes into all its possible rules before asking the systems analyst for the probabilities. In the absence of this refinement I have split the E probability of 5 arbitrarily into a 2 and a 3 for the two sub-tables.

In the next diagram I have taken the transformation through a couple of steps whence the resultant flowchart can be easily imagined.

		5Y		5N			
2Y	2Y	2N	2N	2Y	2Y	2N	2N
1–	1Y	1N	1Y	1N	1Y	1–	1Y
3Y	3–	3Y	3–	3Y	3–	3Y	3–
4Y	4N	4–	4N	4–	4N	4Y	4N
B	E	D	E	C	E	A	E
15	1	10	1	40	1	30	2

In an enlarged version of the flowchart (Fig. 9.1) I have added some statistics. The number below each test is the unit cost of the test. The numbers on the branches indicate, using the given probabilities, the number of cases out of the typical 100 which take the various routes through the chart. It happens in this chart that any route consists of three tests. By multiplying the number by the cost of each test preceding it and then adding the cost of the three tests together we get the cost of all the cases down each of the routes.

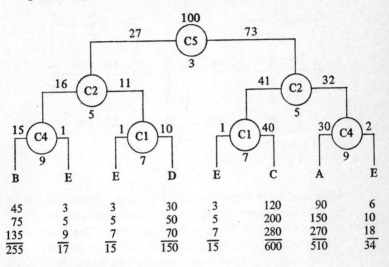

45	3	3	30	3	120	90	6
75	5	5	50	5	200	150	10
135	9	7	70	7	280	270	18
255	17	15	150	15	600	510	34

Total 1596 Ave. 15.96

Fig. 9.1

The sums below the diagram show this arithmetic. The total cost of all 100 cases is 1596, that is an average cost of 15.96.

Please note that it is a different chart from the one developed earlier in the book using weighted dash count and the one for simple dash count. For comparison let us redraw the SDC chart (Fig. 9.2) and supposing that the probabilities are as in the last example let us cost out that chart.

The total cost for the same 100 cases would be 2225, that is average 22.25. So using that chart might have proved in practice much more costly. Furthermore if over the weeks the program is in use the probabilities change we might feel it necessary to re-translate the decision table into a more efficient program.

The optimum solution therefore can be very dependent on the two factors condition cost and rule frequency. Condition cost can be

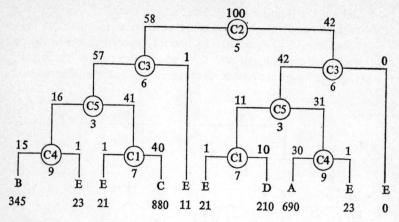

Total 2225 Ave.22.25

Fig. 9.2

minimised by subroutining in the program containing the decision table. Unnecessary repetition of conditions can be taken care of by a very good decision table translator. The frequency of the various rules is data dependent and whilst the translator can make use of frequency information supplied to it, the frequencies may vary in actual fact and the systems analyst must be aware of the likelihood of such changes and advise retranslation of the decision table as appropriate.

10 **The actions**

So far we have concentrated upon the condition half of the table. This was deliberate because in dealing with the conditions lies the best opportunity for optimising the testing sequence. In fact this is because between one condition and another complete independence has been assumed, whereas the conventional attitude towards the actions is that where several have to be performed on the satisfaction of a rule they will be obeyed in the order (top to bottom) that they were written on the table. But more about that later.

Accepting the convention, the things a translator might do are in the main the same things most programmers are familiar with for improving their programs in space and time. Among the action strings following the rules of a decision table there often will be identical ones. Within them there will certainly be similar groups of instructions. The original programmer can of course reduce the number of repeated groups by writing them in the form of sub-routines so that in the decision table they appear as single actions (PERFORM . . . in COBOL terms). This assumes that the programmer knows best. It can happen that there are a variety of ways in which the actions can be grouped. Working out which combinations are first of all possible and then determining which is best, bearing in mind the frequency with which the various groups will be obeyed, is a long and tedious task – just the kind of task we would expect computers to perform for us. This is, then, yet another job which programmers must be prepared to relinquish as soon as decision table preprocessors are good enough.

Conventionally the actions to be performed are marked below their appropriate rule identifiers with an X meaning 'do this' or a blank meaning 'don't do this', and we expect that in the object program the Xs will get attended to in the top to bottom sequence in which they are written in the decision table. We could certainly allow ourselves some freedom here to use various symbols to mean different things in relation to the actions. One preprocessor at least requires a number rather than an X. Actions against which the numbers are the same get performed in the written order, but all actions marked 1 get performed before actions marked 2 which are performed before actions marked 3 and so on.

This could of course save the repetition of actions if some of them appeared in one order in one rule and in a different order in another rule. The biggest advantage, in fact, is that new actions can easily be added to an old table with a minimum of disturbance to the original draft of the table.

Numbers could be used in a different way. They could be used to indicate variations on a basic action. By this we are suggesting an extended numeric mode for the actions very much as we have previously suggested for the conditions.

From table B	5	12	6	
take the Ath element	2	4	23	
and store it in C then	1	2	3	
obey paragraph D	15	18	20	

The above might be the left-hand section of the action part of a decision table. Because of the free English used it is clearly a communication between the systems analyst and programmer. It would be very difficult for a program preprocessor to extract the meaning. The table might have to be accompanied by the various lists (just as in the case of the extended numeric conditions), in this case giving the various B tables, giving the data-names represented by the numerical values of C and the paragraph-names represented by D. The programmer reads the second column as 'from table twelve take the fourth element, store it in the second address given by list C and then obey the eighteenth procedure of list D'.

It is a great pity that the action descriptions and condition descriptions which come naturally to the systems analyst are incomprehensible to the computer. In normal programming this communication gap is bridged to a large extent by programming languages. COBOL can be learnt by analyst and programmer and the whole process speeded up and made proof against misunderstanding by their mutual awareness of how the computer deals with such restricted English. The application of the same disciplines can equally advantageously be applied to decision tables to enable a form of extended table that adds to comprehension while retaining the capability of being processed by computer program. To draft an extended entry table that can be processed automatically we must be aware of how the processor will attribute meaning to what is written. The following example shows that the drafter is familiar with a programming language – in this case, COBOL – and beyond that he is required to remember a simple rule. That is, the processor will regard each condition and each action as an incomplete COBOL phrase. Just where it is incomplete is indicated by the non-COBOL character '?'. The phrase can be made complete by substituting for each '?' the contents of the cell which is on that row and under the appropriate rule identifier.

MOVE ?	FITTER	MINDER	CLEANER	
(?)	GRADE	SHOP	SEX	
TO ?	WK-RATE	WK-RATE	DAY-RATE	
GO TO ?	SKILL-PAY	SEM-SK-PAY	UNSK-PAY	

producing:
MOVE FITTER (GRADE) TO WK-RATE GO TO SKILL-PAY.
MOVE MINDER (SHOP) TO WK-RATE GO TO SEM-SK-PAY.
MOVE CLEANER (SEX) TO DAY-RATE GO TO UNSK-PAY.

It is not difficult for the preprocessor to complete the action statements required to form a perfectly translatable COBOL program. I recommended earlier that we should confine extended entry tables to ones using numerics in the cells but the above discipline which can be applied using many programming languages is an acceptable relaxation of that rule since we have kept control of the semantics.

11 Non-procedural languages

Having, hopefully, put into perspective the subject of translation of decision tables, I should like to return to the point we reached in Chapter 3. We observed that for any particular decision table there were several logically equivalent flow diagrams and this pointed to the fact that the decision table was a more general expression. What had been added to the decision table representation to transform it into one particular flow diagram was an ordering of events. Most programming languages today are procedural languages. That is ones in which the programmer determines the sequence of events in the object program by the sequence in which he writes the statements of the source program. It would be useful to explore the properties of non-procedural languages.

Language processors should have reached such a state of maturity that they are capable of sequencing instructions automatically and doing it better on most occasions than the human programmer. This is difficult for programmers to accept because they often do not appreciate the number of equivalent programs that are possible. Remember that in a program of seven branch levels there are 19×10^{26} different flow diagrams. What a number of possibilities there must be for any sizeable practical problem! The chances of any two programmers writing the same program for a given logical description is infinitely small. The chances of any one programmer getting the best sequence of instructions is also infinitely small. We ought then to examine whether the computer, with its much greater patience, can take over the task of instruction sequencing.

I have shown how storage of tests can be minimised and how obey time through trees of tests can be minimised. In addition there are advantages to be gained in optimising the sequence of the action instructions. In using procedural languages we sometimes by accident try to produce a final result before having calculated an intermediate result. Much more often by carelessness we produce an intermediate result long before it is required in the calculation of the final result and thereby unnecessarily increase the storage requirements. Even though we might be willing to let a piece of software take over the responsibility for sequencing, present languages will not permit us. COBOL, FORTRAN, ALGOL all have an implied rule that, if one source statement precedes another, then the object code derived from the first will be obeyed before the instructions derived from the latter. (Jump instructions are of course exceptions.) It all seems so natural that the manuals don't always bother to point out that it is so. Nor do we often enough bother to consider just how much power this puts in our hands. Without writing a single explicit character, just by the order in which we write the statements, we determine for better or for worse the sequence of instructions in the object program.

If we constructed a program as a collection of statements in which the sequence of the source did not imply the sequence of the object, how difficult would it be to describe the process for sorting them into the right order? You should have no difficulty in sorting the following statement into a sensible order.

> Jehoshaphet begat Joram
> Rehoboam begat Abijah
> Asa begat Jehoshaphet
> Joram begat Uzziah
> Abijah begat Asa

The method is obvious. The statements must be arranged so that the statement containing a name of a son precedes the statement in which that name is used as a father. An exercise that is one degree more difficult but still fairly evident is to put the following statements in a reasonable order.

$$COMPUTE \quad I + C = J$$
$$D \div 7 = E$$
$$G + H = I$$
$$A ** 2 = B$$
$$E \times J = K$$
$$F ** 2 = G$$
$$B \times C = D$$

Each statement has two factors and one result. One possible answer given below was formed simply by arranging that the statement in which a data-name appeared as a result always came somewhere before any statement or statements which used that name as a factor.

$$\begin{aligned}
\text{COMPUTE} \quad A**2 &= B \\
B \times C &= D \\
D \div 7 &= E \\
F**2 &= G \\
G + H &= I \\
I + C &= J \\
E \times J &= K
\end{aligned}$$

We would not have been able to have done that if the programmer had tried to preserve storage space by using the same name for different results obtained at different times. Any automatic program would have had great difficulty in telling how one instance of the name was significantly different from any other. The following program could have been written instead of the previous one in a procedural language and would have given a correct result, but with the statements scrambled and without the procedural rule they could not be sorted without the help of the programmer.

$$\begin{aligned}
\text{COMPUTE} \quad A**2 &= A \\
A \times C &= A \\
A \div 7 &= A \\
F**2 &= F \\
F + H &= F \\
F + C &= F \\
A \times F &= K
\end{aligned}$$

One of the things we must do, then, in trying to shape a non-procedural language is always to use a different identifier for a newly calculated result. It is sometimes the practice to do this in a COBOL program knowing that economy in storage space can be effected later as a separate exercise by REDEFINES added carefully to the data division. Systematic redefinition of data areas should be an operation which could be made automatic.

Sometimes the storage of different values using the same data-names cannot be avoided. For example the storing on separate occasions of the parameters before entry to a subroutine or the updating of an integer which is to be used as a subscript. The programmer might give some assistance.

> ADD 1 AND A GIVING A

> could be

> ADD 1 AND A GIVING A?

where ? meant a later value for A and statements other than this one using A as a factor always preceded this modifying statement. Such practices would certainly help us move to a non-procedural language.

The decision table, we observed, was non-procedural in part, that is in the conditional part, and if we use a non-procedural form of COBOL for the actions that part too could be left for automatic sequencing. Even so such a decision table might seem an odd substitute for a program because it has all its tests at the beginning and all the action statements at the end. But there is no reason why an intelligent preprocessor should not, if there are advantages to be gained, lift some actions up among the conditions. In so doing the rules of precedence must not be broken. We must not for example put an action before a test if the action has only to be performed on the true side and not on the false side. Take for example the following decision table.

```
C1  Y Y N N
C2  Y N - -
C3  - - Y N
A1  X X X X
A2  X X
A3  X   X X
A4    X   X
```

A decision table preprocessor might have offered us the following translation in flowchart form. There are eleven actions to be stored away.

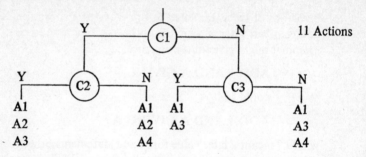

11 Actions

Both branches of the C2 test lead to actions 1 and 2. Supposing always that conditions and actions are not interactive, then A1 and A2 could precede the test C2. Similarly on the other wing A1 and A3 might as well precede C3. But this still leaves A1 on both branches of C1, so A1 could be performed before entering the tree of tests. Here, then, is another flowchart logically equivalent to the previous one but with a need only to store 6 actions.

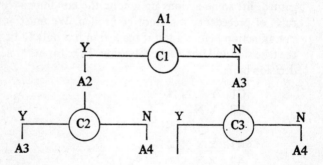

These thoughts add a further complication to choosing the best test sequence. What we might previously have regarded as the best solution judged only on consideration of the condition tests might not be the best taking into account the storage required for the actions. Applying some of the tactics described earlier for deriving the best tree and applying them to one action row alone will be the quickest way to get that action sorted out. This is the same as saying that it will give the arrangement of tests which gets that action highest up the tree. Applying the procedure to the table for each

82

action in turn might give a clue to the best combined arrangement of actions and conditions.

Having by now seen the translation of a decision table into something very much like a normal program we may ask whether it is not possible to represent a whole normal program by one decision table with the hope of producing the optimum object program by automatic means. There are three problems

(1) the sheer size of the undertaking,
(2) the complications usually introduced by over-enthusiastic use of the GO type instruction,
(3) some actions are invariably required before the conditions can be tested and current decision table format does not allow for this.

First the monolithic decision table would almost certainly contain a great many useless cells and the work of translation would be some function of cell number. We cannot expect to be dealing with that ideal program for decision table representation in which all combinations of actions are invoked by all combinations of conditions. A program might for instance read records from a file and process them. The file, say, contains two types of record: goods received notes and invoices. The questions asked and the actions taken on the goods received note might all be quite different from those asked and obeyed for the invoices. Restricting severely the number of conditions and actions the decision table in Fig. 11.1 might be representative of the program.

Invoice Record	Y	Y	Y	Y	N	N	N	N
C2	Y	N	Y	N	–	–	–	–
C3	Y	Y	N	N	–	–	–	–
C4	–	–	–	–	Y	N	Y	N
C5	–	–	–	–	Y	Y	N	N
A1	X	X		X				
A2	X		X					
A3					X	X		X
A4					X		X	X

Fig. 11.1

This one contains 9 × 8 = 72 cells. The natural thing to do would be to test first which type of record has been read and then use one decision table for the goods received note and a separate table for the invoice. This state of affairs is represented by the three tables in Fig. 11.2.

Table 1

Invoice record	Y	N
Go to table 2	X	
Go to table 3		X

Table 2 (invoice)

C2	Y	N	Y	N
C3	Y	Y	N	N
A1	X	X		X
A2	X		X	

Table 3 (Goods received note)

C4	Y	N	Y	N
C5	Y	Y	N	N
A3	X	X		X
A4	X		X	X

Fig. 11.2

This set contains a 2 × 3 = 6 cells, a 4 × 4 = 16 and another 4 × 4 = 16. In all that makes 6 + 16 + 16 = 38 cells – and a good deal less writing and processing. We can, then, simplify the tasks we have been discussing by breaking a large program up into a number of units and handling each unit as a separate decision table. These units can be linked in the way subroutines are used in programs or they can be nested like ALGOL procedures. The advice to be offered on how to sectionalise is exactly the same as would be given on a course on Modular programming. Chapin[3] describes several techniques for reducing the size of decision tables. Of all the arrangements of modules, the carefully nested set is always the easiest to analyse.

The greatest difficulties experienced by all who seek to subject the actual structure of a program to automatic analysis by computer are caused by the GO type instruction. Used indiscriminately it can tie the program into knots which defy flowcharters, precedence adjusters, logic checkers and connectivity analysers alike. An excellent programming discipline that you might try is to write your programs without the use of the GO type instruction, using for control switching the COBOL PERFORM or the FORTRAN DO type instructions. You will find it easier to follow the logic as the program grows. It will be very much easier to maintain and in particular you will be able to see much more clearly the repercussions that modifications to one part of the program cause in another part.

The third problem I mentioned in using one large decision table for a whole program was that in its currently accepted format the decision table does not cater for actions preceding the conditions and it may be that some conditions are testing the results of previous calculations. Either a more sophisticated format must be developed or, better, we should have the sequence of both conditional and imperative statements established by software.

All these proposals are aimed at achieving a single step in the progress of automatic programming – that of freeing the programmer from the onus of instruction sequencing. The form that accomplishment of this objective will take is the specification of a non-procedural language and a translator which will output an optimised procedural version of the same program. If this should strike you as novel, read Lombardi[16] who in 1963 was proposing and implementing just such a language. The chances of success can be increased by confining ones attention to a particular class of programs. Lombardi chose the area of business file handling programs. In that same area of application, ICL's NICOL and IBM's RPG offer languages in which much of the proceduring is implicit rather than explicit. The compiler assumes a basic cycle of events: reading main file, aligning subsidiary files, checking status, processing and output. By 'checking status' I refer to abilities to recognise and signal – control changes, matching keys, record and field types, end-of-file, end-of-run, etc. Essentially, programming consists of declaring how these various states may be recognised and then giving the actions to be performed for each of the possible states. So much of the troublesome part of the logic is provided automatically that program construction time is reduced to a fraction and the number of runs to get a working program is greatly reduced. These languages are more popular on the smaller configurations and are frequently used by people who have had little training in programming. The success they have with practical production of programs is well worth studying by anyone sceptical about non-procedural languages.

The concept of various states with actions associated with those states is common to both these languages and with decision tables, but the formats vary. What the formats enjoy in common is their tabular nature. It is the tabular nature of decision tables which make them easy to understand both by the programmer and by the machine, not the particular format that seems to have become standard. Whilst standardisation has some advantages is would be a pity if experimentation with modified types of tabular formats were hampered. One of the difficulties programmers have in moving from procedural languages to non-procedural languages is their fixation on the flowchart as a preliminary to coding. Flowcharting has become almost a religion where programming is taught and it is regarded as heresy to advocate ways of describing program logic that are radically different. If decision tables were simply prettier descriptions than flowcharts there would be little incentive to become a missionary. It is because they begin to pass the sequencing task to the computer that we must exploit them. But since they are not the complete answer let us continue their development to the complete non-procedural language before their format gets cast in concrete by the standardisers.

12 **In conclusion**

The main part of this book was devoted to a description of the translation of decision tables into procedural languages. The aims were to encourage their use by giving users a background from which they could better evaluate, and therefore cause an improvement in, decision table processors. In Chapter 11 I have tried to show that this is not an end in itself but a means to a greater end, the development of a non-procedural language. I was unable to provide a ready made one but offered some suggestions about contributions that any of us might make to that development. In summary these were

Acquiring better programming habits:
    modular programming,
    avoiding indiscriminate branching,
    new names for new values

Extending the employment of decision tables.

Making decision table processors more sophisticated.

Experimenting with other forms of tabular representation.

Developing non-procedural languages and their compilers.

Developing programs for automatic reassignment of storage.

An ancient Persian poem goes:

> *He who knows not and knows not that he knows not*
>   *is a fool – shun him.*
> *He who knows not and knows that he knows not*
>   *can be taught – teach him.*
> *He who knows and knows not that he knows*
>   *is asleep – wake him.*
> *He who knows and knows that he knows*
>   *is a prophet – follow him.*

The poet never knew that he could have written it as follows

C1	He knows	N	N	Y	Y
C2	He knows C1.	N	Y	N	Y
A1	Shun him.	X			
A2	Teach him.		X		
A3	Wake him.			X	
A4	Follow him.				X

If you found that the suggestions I made in the previous section for further study were too difficult or too trivial or too utilitarian then surely a delightful pastime would be the designing of a processor which could convert decision tables into poetry.

Bibliography

Note: CACM = Communications of the ACM
JACM = Journal of the ACM

[1] Barnard, T. J., 'A new rule mask technique for interpreting Decision Tables', *Comp. Bull.*, 13. 1969.

[2] Canning, 'How to use decision tables', *EDP Analyzer*, May 1966.

[3] Chapin, N., 'Parsing of decision tables', *CACM.*, August 1967.

[4] Chapin, N., 'A guide to decision table utilization', *Data Processing*, Vol. 9, 1967.

[5] CODASYL, 'Proceedings of Symposium on Decision Tables', from *ACM*, September 1962.

[6] Dial, R. B., 'Algorithm 394. Decision table translation', *CACM* September 1970.

[7] Dixon, P., 'Decision tables and their application', *Computer Automation*, April 1964.

[8] Fisher, D. L., 'Data documentation and decision tables', *CACM*, January 1966.

[9] G.I.C.S. Ltd, 'Survey report on the use of decision tables in data processing (U.K.)', for *NCC*, August 1968.

[10] Hawes, M. K., *et al.*, 'Decision table tutorial using DETAB-X', *CODASYL S.D.G.*, 1962.

[11] King, P. J. H., 'Conversion of decision tables to computer programs by rule mask techniques', *CACM*, November 1966.

[12] King, P. J. H., 'Decision tables', *BSC Journal*, 10, 1967.

[13] King, P. J. H., 'Ambiguity in limited entry decision tables', *CACM*, October 1968.

[14] King, P. J. H., 'The interpretation of limited entry decision table format and relationships among conditions', *BSC Journal*, March 1969.

[15] Kirk, H. W., 'Use of decision tables in computer programming', *CACM*, January 1965.

[16] Lombardi, L. A., 'A general business-oriented language based on decision expression', *CACM*, February 1964.

[17] Montalbano, M., 'Tables, flow charts and program logic', *IBM Systems Journal*, September 1962.

[18] Muthukrishnan, C. R. and Rajaraman, V., 'On the conversion of decision tables to computer programs', *CACM*, June 1970.

[19] Pollack, S. L., 'How to build and analyze decision tables', *RAND Corporation*, November 1963.

[20] Pollack, S. L., 'Conversion of limited entry decision tables to computer programs', *CACM*, November 1965.

[21] Press, L. I., 'Conversion of decision tables to computer programs', *CACM*, June 1965.

[22] Reinwald, L. T. and Soland, R. M., 'Conversion of limited entry decision tables to optimal computer programs', *I. JACM*, July 1966; *II. JACM*, October 1967.

[23] Schmidt, O. T. and Kavanagh, T. F., 'Using decision structure tables', *Datamation*, February 1964; March 1964.

[24] Shober, 'Decision tables for better management systems', *Systems & Procedures Journal*, January 1966.

[25] Shwayder, K., 'Conversion of limited entry decision tables to computer programs', *CACM*, February 1971.

[26] Veinott, C. G., 'Programming decision tables in FORTRAN, ALGOL, COBOL', *CACM*, June 1970.

[27] Woodall, A. D., 'A rule mask technique for decision table translation', *BCS Journal*, October 1970.

[28] Evans, O. Y., 'The Evans Table', *Data Processing Digest*, April 1960.

[29] Pollack, S. L., 'Decision Tables: Theory and Practice', J. Wiley & Sons Inc., 1971.

The above book was published after the text for *Programs from Decision Tables* was prepared. It offers in a single volume a comprehensive background to Decision Tables and must therefore be included in the recommended reading on page 2. On page 39 I deplore the lack of any over-view of decision table translation techniques, but I have to acknowledge that this criticism does not apply to *Decision Tables: Theory and Practice* which in its Appendix III has a paper by Marjorie Wiggins which neatly summarises the principal existing approaches. This paper does, however, confirm my opinions that there exists a big gap between the 'quick and nasty' and the 'exhaustive but impractical' approaches.

Index